Living With Post Traumatic Stress Disorder

By

John Ruiz

authorHOUSE™

1663 LIBERTY DRIVE, SUITE 200
BLOOMINGTON, INDIANA 47403
(800) 839-8640
WWW.AUTHORHOUSE.COM

First published by AuthorHouse 09/17/04

ISBN: 1-4184-8085-1 (sc)

Library of Congress Control Number: 2004096227

Printed in the United States of America
Bloomington, Indiana

This book is printed on acid-free paper.

This book is dedicated to those persons who live life swimming upstream, and to those people who know, love and care for them.

TABLE OF CONTENTS

INTRODUCTION

(Advent 2003)

Isaiah 40:31
"but those who wait for the Lord
shall renew their strength, they shall
mount up with wings like eagles,
they shall run and not be weary,
they shall walk and not faint."

It was not until recently that I became aware that a person could be diagnosed with Post-Traumatic Stress Disorder and not have that person walk them through what PTSD meant. How it can work in a person's head and where some of the more difficult twists can lie.

This experience made me ever more grateful to the person who walked (on a number of occasions) with me. Knowing someone with a similar experience was helpful. This truth resurfaced when I was on the other end and explained to a fellow pilgrim who had recently been diagnosed with Post-Traumatic Stress Disorder what had been explained to me. They told me it was helpful and thus I was led to write these words.

The root of Post-Traumatic Stress Disorder is fear that then can cause someone to question his or her own perception of reality. It occurs in a person's life when an experience was simply too much (too traumatic) for a person to process all at one time. In this way, a person protects oneself psychologically the best they can. Protecting one's own identity is an indication of a strong spirit that refuses to be crushed by the weight of one's experience.

At the same time, it also means that a person with Post-Traumatic Stress Disorder carries fear. Fear is a natural human emotion that can be a very helpful gift from God. In some cases, it can lead a person away from dangerous situations and lead a person to self-preservation.

However, fear functions in different ways for a person with PTSD. Since a person with PTSD carries fear then fear can be experienced in situations and at times when it doesn't make sense. When it does not seem appropriate for what a person is experiencing in the moment. In other situations, when fear is a normal response to outside circumstances a person with PTSD can experience the initial (normal) sensation which can be followed by a back-up layer. Together this can be difficult and again it can get a person to question their own perception of reality because a person might feel that they are over-reacting. Thus a person can start believing there is something "wrong" with them.

In both cases, it is important for the person with PTSD to remind oneself that there is nothing wrong with them. They are simply experiencing reality in a way that is NORMAL for a person who lives life with Post-Traumatic Stress Disorder.

I have learned that talking with another or simply thinking or writing can be very helpful in sorting out why I felt the way I felt. At the same time, it must be said, that I can't always determine why I felt the way I felt. If I could, then I wouldn't have Post-Traumatic Stress Disorder. Those with PTSD carry fear and sometimes it is not possible to identify why latent fear may have surfaced. In these situations, "it is what it is", is a source of wisdom.

As one can imagine, living with a person with PTSD can be different and at the same time difficult. However, with knowledge comes understanding and with understanding comes healing for all concerned.

Post-Traumatic Stress Disorder can be very challenging in a number of ways. First, is the function of fear it self. When a person is at a point of growth a person is vulnerable. We see this over and over again when we observe nature.

In this way, growth and vulnerability are natural. Further, it is natural for a person to experience moderate levels of fear when they feel vulnerable. However, for a person with PTSD times of personal growth, which are naturally accompanied by a sense of vulnerability, can also be accompanied by a large (latent) surge of fear.

When in the face of a large surge of fear it is natural for a person to respond with the instinct of fight or flight. A way of responding that, at times, can be a gift from God. However, a surge of fear that does not seem appropriate to a person's experience. In this way, a person with PTSD can develop a mindset where they do not want to experience surges of fear so they respond by trying to protect oneself with solitude or only participating in "safe" social settings or even attempting to withdraw from times and situations of personal growth.

I have learned that developing clarity in one's mind during these times has been very helpful. In these situations, clarity has reassured me that I am John and I am okay. Also, on a few occasions, clarity has allowed me to channel the latent energy into the adventures and challenges of the day. In this way, the channeled energy has proved to be a strong motor and a source of unexpected energy reserve.

Again, this might be unusual for loved ones to be around since points of personal growth can be accompanied by times of increased anxiety within the loved one with PTSD. However, with knowledge comes understanding and with understanding comes healing for all concerned.

Finally, there are times when a person with PTSD can be misdiagnosed with being Paranoid or having Multiple Personalities. While this can be the lot in life that some people live with, it is not a necessary reality for a person with PTSD.

A person with PTSD is not paranoid because paranoia is rooted in groundless fear. This is not true for a person with PTSD for there is a real experience that produced fear that one carries and can surface at different times. Therefore, developing clarity or simply accepting the experience of fear allows the person with PTSD to accept oneself and their own perception of reality.

Living life with multiple personalities is not a necessary reality for a person with PTSD. Family members and close associates might experience it in a similar way to this because to development of clarity or acceptance can function like a "switch" in one's mind. Where a person can seem distant or anxious or tired and them all of a sudden they are not anymore. This occurs inside one's head when a person finally sorts out why they felt the way they felt or the latent energy simply fades away or when a person simply accepts the person they are and that they are okay.

For me this is one of the fruits of faith because God breathes life into all persons; including me. In this way, the assurance that I am okay does not have to come from me but comes from the One who has created and gives life.

"With knowledge comes understanding and with understanding comes healing for all concerned."

God Bless,
John Ruiz

(Spring 2003)

How do you explain to another person that there are times that noises can sound unusually loud? That at times certain pitches can feel like a toothache and simply hurt. How can you explain that the natural energy and spontaneity of the teachable moment, which was one of the things that attracted you to a teaching career is also one of the reasons you realized you were no longer able to pursue that career and be the teacher you wanted to be?

How do you explain to someone that there are times when your nerves act up? Sometimes it's because of what is going on in life and sometimes you have no idea why your nerves are acting up? Most times this occurs at night when you wake up disoriented, not sure where you are and you simply need to take in your surroundings to remind yourself where you are. How do explain that times like these are frequently accompanied by a race to the bathroom? What impact might this have on personal relationships? One can never know. One can only know that as anything else, it is a part of the whole.

How do you tell another that you have to be aware of certain stomach twinges? That there are times you simply have to stop everything to get to the bathroom. That you are not proud of the fact that you have had two accidents in your adult life and a number of near misses. But you simply have become aware of certain twinges so you can cope the next time it happens.

How do you tell another that there have been times when you would lie in bed and look at your hands because it felt like energy was pulsating in them? And you needed to look at your hands to see if they were moving but they were not. So you rub the tops of your fingers with your thumb or make a fist a few times just to reassure yourself with a "normal" sensation.

How do you tell someone that this energy creates a desire (need) for structure and clear, consistent expectations in work and one's personal life? And when these expectations change or are given in contradictory ways it feeds into latent energy and might leak out in passive aggressive ways. How do you cope in new ways and forgive yourself when it becomes clear that this reality has happened and you are not a victim therefore you had a role in difficult situations? Thus needing to grow and find new ways of expressing oneself and coping.

How do you tell someone that if you really focus on a person's breathing or voice inflection it can almost always tell you if anger and frustrations are lying under the surface and will simply come your way? That you had come to learn this was simply your role, your function in a unit. How do you say that to another person without people thinking you are odd?

How do you cope when you finally realize that not everyone's head is the same? It is strange but also okay. And there are times when you wonder how other people can survive without knowing some of the basics. For example, when faced with an un-winnable situation or impossible task you need to stand tall and become invisible at the same time, or the knowledge to always defend oneself in the face of strong anger.

What I have tried to explain is part of my life. I see it as neither a good or bad thing because it simply is the way things have always been. At age 34 I found out this is called Post-Traumatic Stress Disorder. Knowing it had a name and there are resources, people and ways to cope differently has been a very challenging and healing experience.

The meditations that follow in this book were written from or near this place. For it is one of my intersection points. The Christian faith is a living faith, a personal journey, because there are countless intersection points between faith, experience, scripture and the witness of others. Sometimes these intersection points can be shared, like the shared experience of the towers coming down. Sometimes an intersection point can be very personal, an experience that is hard to explain or the birth of a child. There are countless intersection points and Post-Traumatic Stress Disorder is one of my intersection points.

When I first accepted this as part of who I am and what my reality is like it was extremely healing. This led to additional points of healing when others accepted me and did not treat me differently because I have a label that can be associated with my name.

It is very important to state that Post-Traumatic Stress Disorder does not define me but it is part of me therefore a part of my reality.

In this way, the meditations that follow were written out of this intersection point. Either at that personal time in life or preaching out of or near that place because life circumstances were placing me near or in some of these personal challenges or struggles.

It is my hope and prayer that this book might bring healing and insight to those who might be able to relate to these intersection points. Relating in personal ways or knowing someone that these intersection points might relate too.

Finally, the book tries to model how faith and the journey of faith has been a positive thing in my life. How faith is real and how it has added life to life in countless ways and in many difficult situations.

God Bless

SWIMMING UPSTREAM AND THE REALNESS OF FAITH

(Spring 2001)

My name is John Ruiz and I am a Christian man with a condition called Post-Traumatic Stress Disorder. This is simply a record of different ways that my faith has helped me over the years, at various times and in various situations in my life. It is hoped that through the sharing of these meditations, which were written over many years, as were the meditations found in my first book, <u>A Message of Life and Love: Proclaiming Good News from a Johannine Perspective</u>, that people will have a better understanding of life lived within these realities. And finally, the hope, life and renewal that continually embraces us in the context of Christian faith.

As I am writing this introduction and putting together this book I am a few months past my 36th birthday. And it is strange as I look back. I see faith as a gift, since for me it became very real at an early age, probably between ages 5-8. In this way, I realize now, I was able to develop opposing viewpoints of my own self-identity. Some viewpoints that I carry with me are very negative, and others, especially those that come from faith, offer a different perspective. Therefore, even while I was growing up, I was aware of internal struggles that go on inside my head. These struggles (at times) can feel like they go on all the time.

It was not until I became a father that I realized the potential to continue the cycle with my own children. When this occurred I was horrified and I re-dedicated myself to an earlier vow that the cycle would end with me.

It is difficult to know how one thing can affect another. It is only safe to state that one thing does affect another. Therefore, one is aware that these experiences affected other areas of life. There were times when repressed emotions would "leak" out in various ways; at times in unexpected tearful emotions, or unexplainable moments of anxiety, or impulses to outbursts of anger (that needed to be controlled), or times

3

when noises were inappropriately loud, or times of mild depression and fatigue.

This is not to say that life was bad. Life is good! It is simply stating a reality. Further, I will discuss at length in later portions of this book how it is not accurate, fair or helpful to identify oneself as either a hero or a victim. Since both forms of self-identification do not lead one to a foundation of hope, love and renewal.

For a little over 34 years these various realities, joys and struggles were simply a part of life. And finding out that it had a name, Post-Traumatic Stress Disorder, and there are people and miracles of modern medication that can assist you was both helpful and challenging on many different levels.

For nearly seven years, I attempted to shield my children and family from tendencies I knew dwelled within. Then for a little over a year I tried with all my energy and resources to end the cycle and get rid of it! Only to realize during one difficult weekend in January 2001 that the best I could do was accept it.

That, somehow, accepting my Post-Traumatic Stress Disorder and the tendencies that dwell within would I not allow it to affect me as much as it had in the past. Initially, this realization was very depressing. And for a few days I needed help working with self- images.

I was okay developing the image of an illness. However, my vocabulary was indicating an image like the flu. In this way, I was realizing that if I walked into a room then someone with an illness walked into the room. It would then follow that if I had something like the flu then I might give my illness to them by simply walking into the room. This added to my depression.

However, through prayer, writing and talking to another, I was able to recognize the errors in my image and develop a new one. The truth is, when I walk into a room, a person with an illness does walk into that room. However, it is an illness like diabetes, not the flu. In this way, it is always a part of me but I would not give it away by simply walking in the room.

This realization would lead to the most healing experience in this journey called life. On a Sunday evening in January, a little over a month before my 36th birthday, I gathered my children, now ages 8 and 10, and told them that dad takes various medications everyday. I showed them the pills and told them why I take each one and why there are times when their dad needed to go away for a little while to get things together. I then concluded, by noting how grateful I was that God provides us with people and medicines that can make are lives better.

They were difficult moments. And then the healing came. For each of my children in their own way, after asking the questions they needed to ask, said "okay!" I was still simply dad! They did not see me any differently!

These gifts allowed me to share with others, at later times, and again be met with kindness and understanding. This would lead to further healing and a growing acceptance.

I would learn a short time later that one of the reasons it was so difficult to determine the moment of my Post-Traumatic Stress Disorder is that it is simply the way things have always been. I am not able to locate a specific moment or experience, as in most cases, when a person did not know this reality as a part of their life until a certain experience happened and then after that experience it was now a part of their life story.

Finally, I want to state emphatically that, "I am not a victim!" In fact, to label me in this way really ticks me off!

Let me explain. Early experiences can make life challenges and adventures more difficult.

Further, in reality, one must (at times) painfully recognize that early experiences have probably contributed in various ways in creating real life challenges.

John Ruiz

However, this does not mean a person is a victim! It does not define oneself and one is only a victim if one allows such experiences to define one's personhood.

Therefore, while these early experiences can influence and continue to influence one's life in various ways, it does not dictate *how* one chooses to encounter life's challenges and adventures. This includes those challenges that might have been caused in various ways, unless one lets it. If one allows these difficult realities in one's life to dictate how one encounters life then one has defined oneself as a victim.

If one chooses to "swim upstream" and claim for oneself *how* one will encounter life, then one is not a victim. One is there own person. And the possibilities for joy, love and freedom in this life can be touched.

For me the gifts that gave me these insights have come from my Christian faith. These gifts would include personal experiences, experiences of other faithful Christians who in a variety of ways have blessed my life, and the gift of scripture; which invites and welcomes our personal encounter and dialogue.

May the words that follow be a source of understanding and healing.

Amen

FOR WE ARE ONE BODY IN CHRIST

I Corinthians 12:12-31a

For just as the body is one and has many members, and all the members of the body, though many, are one body, so it is with Christ. For in the one Spirit we are all baptized into one body-Jews or Greeks, slaves or free - and we are all made to drink of the one Spirit.

Indeed, the body does not consist of one member but many. If the foot would say, "Because I am not a hand, I do not belong to the body," that would not make it any less a part of the body. And if the ear would say, "Because I am not an eye, I do not belong to the body," that would not make it any less a part of the body.

If the whole body were an eye, where would the hearing be? If the whole body were hearing, where would the sense of smell be? But as it is, God arranged the members of the body, each one of them, as he chose.
If all were a single member, where would the body be?

As it is, there are many members, yet one body. The eye cannot say to the hand, "I have no need of you" nor again the head to the feet, "I have no need of you." On the contrary, the members of the body that seem to be weaker are indispensable, and those members of the body that we think less honorable we clothe with greater honor, and our less respectable members are treated with greater respect, whereas our more respectable members do not need this.

But God has so arranged the body, giving the greater honor to the parts that lacked it, so that there may be no dissension within the body, but the members may have the same care for one another. If one member suffers, all suffer together with it; if one member is honored, all rejoice together with it.

Now you are the body of Christ and individually members of it. And God has appointed in the church first apostles, second prophets, third teachers; then deeds of power, then gifts of healing, forms of assistance, forms of leadership, various kinds of tongues.

Are all apostles?
Are all prophets? Are all teachers?
Do all work miracles? Do all possess gifts of healing?
Do all speak in tongues? Do all interpret?
But strive for the greater gifts.
And I will show you a still more excellent way.

Meditation

(A Time of Healing: January 2001)

The apostle Paul writes today's passage. And it is a passage that talks about the many parts that make up the body of Christ. It talks about how each part is important for the whole and how no one gift should be esteemed over another.

The theologian Renita Weems writes, "God imparts insights and gifts not for the benefit of any individual, but for contributing to the common good."[1]

Journeying to Estonia last summer reminded me once again that the Body of Christ is always a little more vast and a little more beautiful than we imagine.[2]

This occurs as we allow ourselves to meet each other, not as we expect them to be, but as they are. It also occurs when we allow ourselves to meet ourselves as who we are, both the parts of ourselves that we like and the parts of ourselves we do not like.

I think I told the story of Sherri once before. Sherri was someone I met only once and actually knew for only about half an hour yet she has made a lasting impression on me. And she continues to challenge me to meet each other, not as we might expect them to be, but rather as they are.

It was while I was a pastor of youth and young adults in Westerville, Ohio and we had developed a young adults ministry called YACHT clubs (Young Adult Christians Hanging Together). As a group we traveled to be with people at a Ronald MacDonald House near Children's Hospital. On two occasions we brought sloppy Joes, sang praise music

---

[1] Renita J. Weems, *New Proclamation: Year C, 2000-01: Advent through Holy Week* (Fortress Press: Minneapolis) 2000, p. 98.
[2] The World Methodist Evangelism Institute of the World Methodist Council titled *Jesus Christ: The Heart and Soul of Evangelism: Communicating The Gospel Today* was held August 7-14, 2000 in Tallinn, Estonia.

and visited. Each time the people staying at the Ronald MacDonald House seemed to enjoy the dinner, the company and joined in the praise singing.

One evening, I noticed that every table had more than one person except one. At this table sat a woman, alone, with a note pad. She was an unassuming woman wearing black-framed glasses and had tattoos on her arms. At first impression one might not expect to find a woman of vast internal resources and Christian conviction.

Yet she was. For as we visited I became amazed at this unassuming woman, wearing black-framed glasses and tattoos and sitting alone with a pad of paper at a Ronald MacDonald House. For she was attempting to write a note to the birth mother of Noah, a young child she and her husband were adopting. Noah was a special needs child. And she had been at the house for nine days because Noah had been born with water on the brain. Noah would be the seventh special needs child she and her husband adopted. During the conversation she talked about her husband and children, her church, and how impressed she was that a few of the college students were signing songs. Somehow I got the feeling someone down the road might hear of an idea to have sign language incorporated into church worship. Allowing ourselves to meet each other can lead to unexpected insights.

This can also happen as we allow ourselves to meet ourselves as we are. Even the parts we do not like.

My favorite image concerning this idea comes from the book A Portrait of Jesus written by Joseph Girzone. In this book Girzone writes, "Jesus' love is not superficial or fickle. Friendship doesn't end just because we do stupid things, especially out of our weakness. It's all right! All Jesus' friends limp or are seriously defective in some way. It doesn't bother Him. That is what is so extraordinary about God's love."[3]

3 Joseph F. Girzone, *A Portrait of Jesus* (Doubleday: New York, London, Toronto, Sydney, Auckland) 1998, p. 28-29.

I love this small passage, yet at the same time we must be very careful in today's American culture not to glamorize the things that make us limp. They might be a part of us yet they do not define us. And many times the things that can make us limp are not experienced in glamorous ways at all.

Further, in our American culture we must be very careful not to rally around a victimization mentality, that either wants to, again, glamorize a situation or at the other extreme condone any form of behavior due to ones situation in life. Whatever that situation in life might be.

As someone who works on a daily basis to cope with stress, and at times depression, due to childhood trauma and verbal abuse, these concepts are very important. For it is a part of the person I am. As much as I might not like that fact, I have recently learned that only by accepting it as part of the person that I am, will I be able to accept the ways I might limp, and not allow my Post-Traumatic Stress Disorder to affect me and the people I meet along this journey called life as much as it has in the past.

It's kind of strange. I worked and coped with this reality (with various degrees of success and failures) for 34 years before I knew it had a name. And for the last year and a half learning it has a name, that there are people and medications God provides that can help has been very a challenge on many different levels.

For God is God at all times and in all places. And God Loves Us For Who We Are; Who We Can Become and by God's Grace, Who We Are Becoming…

Praise God!

Amen

2 TIMOTHY

2 Timothy 3:14-4:5

*But as for you, continue in what you have learned
and have been convinced of, because you know from whom
you learned it, and how from infancy you have known the holy
scriptures, which are to make you wise for salvation through
Jesus Christ.*

*All scripture is God-breathed and is useful for teaching,
rebuking, correcting, and training in righteousness, so that
everyone who belongs to God may be thoroughly equipped for
every good work.*

*In the presence of God and Christ Jesus, who will judge the
living and the dead, and in view of his appearing and his
kingdom, I give you this charge:*

*Preach the Word; be prepared in season and out of season;
correct, rebuke and encourage-with great patience and careful
instruction.*
*For the time will come when people will not put up with sound
doctrine.*
*Instead to suit their own desires, they will gather around them a
great number of teachers to say what their itching ears want to
hear.*
*They will turn their ears away from the truth and turn aside to
myths.*

*But you, keep your head in such situations, endure hardships, do
the work of the evangelist, discharge the duties of your ministry.*

Meditation

(Traveling through this adventure called life: January 1996)

Delivered during worship at the Methodist Theological School in Ohio shortly before graduation.

I am going to begin with a story. This story is about a young man. Little is known of this young man's early years, except he was raised primarily by his mother and grandmother and these persons taught him of the faith through deed and instruction in the scriptures. The young boy took to the scriptures and modeled after his mother and grandmother in faith.

One day, the young person met a man who would become a teacher, mentor and friend. In fact, he became a father figure to the young person. The two grew in friendship. Eventually, the man, whose work meant he traveled a lot, asked the now young man to join him on a journey. The young man agreed and through many journeys and the teachings of his mentor he grew in self-confidence and faith. The young man remembers those days fondly.

But today things do not seem as clear. The young man is seeking clarity and direction in his life. He has not seen his aging mentor for a while. And he has heard strange stories revolving around the man.

It seems the old man has found himself in jail. Again! The crusty old man sure could be cantankerous and stubborn. That he knew from first hand experience. But wasn't that unflinching faithfulness and unashamed zeal what attracted him to the old man in the first place?

And what about his friends who had also followed the old teacher? Friends who he heard now followed new ideas and new teachers. The young man was struggling. What should he do? And how should he do it? Should he go and see his "father" friend in jail? Rumor has it the old man may be close to death. Or should he join the others and move on to new understandings and ideas? Ideas that seemed much more pleasing to the ear. In fact, one might say they were ideas of the day arising from the day's times.

In the midst of all this uncertainty the young man gets a letter. He opens it. He pauses upon reading who it is from. The letter is from that stubborn, unflinchingly faithful old man. The letter is from Paul.

This scripture passage is from 2 Timothy. A letter that the theologian Luke Timothy Johnson in his book <u>The Writings of the New Testament: An Interpretation</u> suggests is a pastoral letter of love and commitment that is addressed to Timothy.[1] Timothy, who throughout the Pauline epistles, is mentioned very fondly. Timothy it seems is a faithful follower. But he can be shy at times and uncertain, and maybe even on occasion hard to get along with.

It is Timothy that this letter is written too. A letter written while in jail and at a time when Paul's age and health are catching up with him. 2 Timothy 6-8, which immediately follows this passage reads, "For I am already being poured out like a drink offering, and the time has come for my departure. I have fought the good fight, I have finished the race, I have kept the faith. Now there is in store for me the crown of righteousness, which the Lord, the righteous, will award to me on this day-and not only to me, but also to all who have longed for his appearing."

It is in this context that Paul is writing this letter of love, encouragement, instruction and commitment. Paul having fought the good fight, finished the race and having kept the faith is writing to a beloved friend; possibly someone who he saw as a son.

What would you write and say to someone? What would you most want to give or instruct to a child or grandchild, brother or sister, spouse or friend? What would you most

[1] Luke Timothy Johnson, *The Writings of the New Testament: An Interpretation* (Fortress Press: Philadelphia) 1986, p. 391-396.

want that person to hold onto when they are faced with the struggles of life? Struggles that one day soon you may not be able to struggle together for one's time is drawing near and one can sense the loving God of grace and mercy calling you home.

Let us turn to our scripture and see what St. Paul says to his beloved young friend, Timothy.

First, we find in this passage which serves as a type of summary for this letter instruction to "continue in what you have learned and have become convinced of, because you know from whom you learned it, and how from infancy you have known the holy scriptures which are able to make you wise for salvation through Jesus Christ."

Notice that Paul is reminding Timothy of his upbringing and the faith of his mother and grandmother who taught him in faith and in the scriptures. In 2 Timothy 1:5 we learn that the mother's name is Eunice and the grandmother's name is Lois. What a challenge to us to share the faith through deed, faith and instruction with those little ones we know and are entrusted in our care.

Second, within this instruction, Paul is exhorting Timothy to draw upon his own experiences and the realness of faith and God's presence in his life. In other words, Paul is instructing Timothy to draw upon those times when "while smiling God called out his name."[2]

We, like Timothy, must claim our own experiences for they validate the realness of the experience and the working of God in our lives. We all have experiences. I believe we have all heard God smiling and calling out our name.

[2] Cesareo Gabarain writes the hymn "Lord You Have Come to the Lakeshore". Gertrude C. Suppe, George Lockwood and Raquel Gutierrez-Achon translate it. It is hymn #344 in The United Methodist Hymnal (The United Methodist Publishing House: Nashville, Tennessee) 1989.

So what are your precious experiences? Maybe a time in your life when a door opened when before there was only a wall and you know the liberating, empowering experience of walking through that door. Possibly, a time when you were caught so much within yourself and your own talents that you neglected God only to have God's gracious hand touch you and save you once again. A time when you quietly held the hand of a loved one who was ailing or near death and in prayer laid them into God's loving arms and then recognized God's presence and comforting peace. Possibly a time of utter joy, like the time you held your child in your hands and thanked God for the gift of life and knew that your life was forever changed in a blessed way for the gift of this little one entrusted to your care.

Or a time of absolute grief and weeping when in despair and anger you roared at God, "Why!" Only to realize in your pain you were not alone, that Jesus was weeping with you and gently breathing life back into your aching soul.

We all have our own precious experiences. And we, like Timothy, are instructed to lay claim to our experiences of faith in the God of love and grace.

Third, Paul is drawing Timothy to the scriptures. The scriptures that Paul claims are God breathed. Meaning that through the scriptures one is able to encounter the living presence of God who is continually breathing God's spirit and life into God's word. It is in the scriptures that Paul instructs one will find correct training in righteousness, elements for teaching and foundations for rebuking.

Fourth, Paul is instructing Timothy to model, to model himself. What a glorious day it would be if one day one would speak of us, that we have fought the good fight, finished the race and kept the faith. And we, like Paul, have in store for us the crown of righteousness which the Lord, the righteous judge will save.

Finally, and foremost Paul is instructing Timothy to model Christ. 2 Timothy 2:8-9 reads, "Remember Jesus Christ, raised from the dead, descended from David. This is my gospel, for which I am suffering even to the point of being chained like a common criminal." Timothy, like us, is instructed to lean upon God. For God will not fail us.

Within this letter Paul also, like any loving caretaker would, tries to identify any hurdles and hardships that this young friend will encounter. I can really identify with this. Don't we all want to tell those in our care the hazards they will know? And hope that because of our instructions these hurdles may not seem so high and the hardships not so harsh. Within this loving context Paul identifies hurdles and hardships and how to handle oneself within these difficult situations.

One of the great challenges of our day is the difficulty of sharing and giving our faith in God to all persons. To follow Paul's exhortation to do the work of the evangelist. I am going to pause for a moment to give some time to this struggle because it is a struggle we as Christian communities are engulfed in.

Before I begin to analyze today's struggles in Christian evangelism I need to define what it is. This is because often we only think of evangelism as someone standing up, getting red in the face, shouting and pounding the Bible on the pulpit a time or two for dramatic effect. While this is a plausible voice within the Christian community it is not the only plausible and effective voice. For many times evangelism is very quiet and patient.

A definition of evangelism that I would like to propose is simply those times when I as a Christian, individually or collectively, pause and look out at the world and ponder how to give God away. It is attempting to live out Jesus' teaching, "Freely you have received, now freely give" (Matthew 10:8b).

What occurs if we never, as individuals and as churches, collectively do this? What happens, if for whatever reason, our evangelical voice becomes silent and we allow an evangelical vacuum to develop and linger? What will both those persons inside the church and those currently not being served by the church conclude and feel?

They will conclude and feel one of three things.

The first conclusion is, "It must not be that important."

Second, "It is something we should not do. We should not burden others with faith."

Third, the conclusion that "we Christians do not have anything unique to say. Nothing unique to offer."

And those, then, who see themselves within the Christian community, will all too often begin to see themselves as the saved within the saved.

The question then becomes, "Why if these are the tragic consequences of an evangelical vacuum is it so difficult for us to do? Why is it that so many of the evangelical perspectives that make up the Christian evangelical voice so often, silent?"

The first difficulty to Christian evangelism in our day is the issue, "What do I say?" "What is our collective voice?" This occurs because there are many collective voices with scriptural integrity within our Christian communities, and the development of many collective voices has resulted in the difficulty for any of them to uplift their voice boldly, and the result is, all too often, the creation of an evangelical vacuum.

For this reason I would like to uplift one collective evangelical voice, the one I reside in, and encourage with a sense of urgency others to uplift their own collective evangelical voice if it differs from the one I will present.

Let me explain. One of the four life-changing classes I had the privilege to be a part of within my seminary education was a course on evangelism taught by the President of Trinity Lutheran Seminary in Columbus, Ohio, Bishop Anderson. Bishop Anderson is a wonderful teacher and the structure of his class was to present the questions one must answer within

Christian evangelism. The two under-pinning questions that then allows one to enter into various new questions.

He began the class by stating that we are going to be answering two questions. First, "Does Jesus make a difference?" And second, "What difference does Jesus make?" Then he paused and I remember thinking, "Yes! Finally, an easy seminary class!" And then he finished by saying that if you are already working on the second question, then you never answered the first.[3]

You see within Christian evangelism the question, "Does Jesus make a difference?" is the question. If one does not answer this question, if we do not collectively answer this question and present it to the communities we serve we then create an evangelical vacuum. Further, we reflect three possible conclusion: it must not be that important, it is something we should not do, or we as Christians have nothing unique to say and offer.

A collective evangelical voice that can emerge within this road proclaims as one's foundation, "We affirm the potential for God's salvific will beyond Jesus Christ because of Jesus Christ. And what the Christian has to freely give within God's salvific will is the Divine Son, Jesus Christ."

The second difficulty within Christian evangelism that we struggle to address in our day is the issue of *TIME*. I would suggest that the issue of time is the defining challenge of Christians of this generation. When will persons, both young and old, have time to experience Christian community and fellowship? When will persons of this day, both young and old, have the time to pursue Biblical insights? When will persons, both young and old, have the time to bow in prayer? When in our day will persons have the opportunity to experience the God of love and grace and grow in love and faith in God?

[3] Dennis A. Anderson, Course Evangelism MN 2604, taught at Trinity Lutheran Seminary in Columbus, Ohio during the Fall, Quarter 1994.

If we remember in this scripture passage, Paul initially reminds Timothy of his upbringing and the faith he has known and been witnessed to from his infancy. Then Paul exhorts Timothy to draw upon his own experiences and the realness of God in his life.

In today's culture, God continues to touch persons and woos them into God's presence, but all too often persons do not recognize the quiet, loving touch of God in their lives. They may go years and even a lifetime trying to unravel and make sense out of an experience in their lives; a feeling of presence that they cannot define. They cannot make sense out of it. But the realness of the experience exists and the inability to know and claim the fullness of the experience haunts them. This is God, graciously touching their lives as God has so wonderfully touched your life and mine. But many times the person has no reference point. They have no foundation upon which they can lay that experience because they have not been embraced by a foundation of Christian community and love. And for this reason, many times people are unable to claim the experience of God actively reaching out to them in their lives and they drift in restless wanting.

Why does this occur in such a dramatic way in our day and in our culture? The reason is the growing separation of state and faith in our society. Our society is one in which the lines between culture and faith are becoming more and more defined. This is not a condemnation of our culture but rather an attempt to accurately define the challenges that exist for Christians of this day. The lines between culture and faith are more defined today than they were even a few short years ago.

One quick example, on many occasions I go for lunch to Wendys to get a single and fry. It was about a month ago while having lunch that I noticed something rather odd. I noticed that the soundtrack in the restaurant was playing Christmas songs. But then I realized that none of the songs made any reference to Jesus or to Christianity in general. Oh, there were lively songs, Little Richard singing "Jingle Bells" and Neil Diamond singing "Santa Claus is Coming to Town" to name a few. But there were no songs mentioning Jesus. No, "Silent Night" or "Away in a Manger". Jesus was removed from the music of the season and had been replaced by secular songs of an X-mass season.

You may be wondering, "Well that is not a very big deal! So what?" Yet it is a big deal, for it marks one of the dramatic shifts within our culture as we separate culture and God.

I can remember as a young boy, no more than twenty years ago, saving five or ten dollars and going to Scotts to buy Christmas presents for my sister, brother and mom. I wasn't forgetting my dad but all us kids realized dad would somehow be disappointed come Christmas morning if we kids had not pulled our resources to buy him his annual big bottle of Brute after-shave.

I can remember walking up and down the aisles of Scotts trying to locate the perfect presents. I would hear the music in the store. Going up and down the aisles I would hear "Silent Night" or "O Come all Ye Faithful". I would be humming the songs and a special kind of bounce would fill my heart and the spirit of Christmas engulfed me.

This was my experience growing up and maybe you experienced a similar experience growing up in your own little town. But these will not be the experiences of my children as they one day go out to buy Christmas gifts for their mom and dad. It will not be their experience because the lines between culture and faith have become ever increasingly defined. And the challenge, the great challenge of this generation is "How will we as Christian communities collectively respond?"

How will we engage our society and ensure the time required for an individual, young or old, to have experiences of Christian community and faith, to be engulfed by the spirit of God within our communities? So that when God so beautifully touches lives, as God will, people will have the foundation and the experience necessary to realize and claim the hand of God in their lives, freely and graciously wooing them into God's presence.

Finally, a concluding thought. I would like to share an image that has emerged from my seminary experience at, The Methodist Theological School in Ohio. We have probably all seen the picture of Jesus knocking on the door. As I entered seminary I had always heard it explained that this is a picture demonstrating Jesus knocking and our willingness to open the door and welcome Jesus in.

In seminary, I heard a powerful new twist explaining this picture. It was explained to me that the picture of our Lord knocking is not only one in which we are inviting Jesus in but also one in which Jesus is calling us out.

Both of these are powerful images and a third has developed and challenged my heart and mind. In this image, in this picture, Jesus is standing about to knock on the door. Only as one looks closer at the picture one realizes that the one poised to knock on the door is us, in representative ministry for Jesus, our Lord and Savior. And standing poised to knock, but in reality we are only standing poised, but not knocking we recognize God smiling and calling out to us, "When? When my children? When will you knock in my name?"

Amen

THE STARFISH DANCE

Matthew 13:24-30

Jesus told them another parable:
"The kingdom of heaven is like a man who sowed good seed in
his field.
But while everyone was sleeping, his enemy came and sowed
weeds among the wheat, and went away. When the wheat
sprouted and formed heads, then the weeds also appeared.

The owner's servants came to him and said,
"Sir, didn't you sow good seed in your field? Where then did the
weeds come from?"

" 'An enemy did this,' he replied.

"The servants asked him,
'Do you want us to go and pull them up?'

" 'No," he answered, 'because while you are pulling the weeds,
you may root up the wheat with them.
Let both grow together until the harvest. At that time I will tell
the harvesters:
First collect the weeds and tie them in bundles to be burned;
then gather the wheat and bring it into the barn."

Matthew 13:36-43

Then he left the crowd and went into the house.
His disciples came to him and said,
"Explain to us the parable of the weeds in the field."

He answered,
"The one who sowed the good seed is the Son of Man.
The field is the world, and the good seed stands for the children
of the kingdom.

The weeds are the children of the evil one, and the enemy who sows them is the devil.
The harvest is the end of the age, and the harvesters are angels.

"As the weeds are pulled up and burned in the fire, so it will be in the end of the age. The Son of Man will send out his angels, and they will weed out of his kingdom everything that causes sin and all who do evil.
They will throw them into the fiery furnace, where there will be weeping and gnashing of teeth. Then the righteous will shine like the sun in the kingdom of the Father.
Let anyone with ears listen!"

Meditation

(Traveling through this adventure called life: Fall 1996)

This is one of those parables told by Jesus that has something we can all relate to. I am sure that many, if not all of us, at some time have worked the soil and planted seeds. Hopeful that something good to eat or beautiful to see would develop. Perhaps you anticipated the ripe tomatoes that you would place on that hamburger or in that salad. Or, as I like them best, simply sliced on a plate with a little salt and pepper. Perhaps the seeds you planted were that of flowers; irises or tulip bulbs or mums and you looked forward to that exciting touch of spring when that flower would begin to emerge from the ground, develop into a bud and brilliantly burst into beauty.

You can probably tell I have a little gardener, slash farmer, in me. And this makes this parable of Christ seem odd. For I am sure that all of us who have attempted to grow something know the persistence of weeds. In fact, sometimes as we grow those seeds we might wonder if we are growing weeds or growing green beans. And if we want green beans then we had better do some weeding. This makes this parable seem odd.

This parable is odd and therefore it is difficult. The scripture, as recorded in the gospel of Matthew, describes even the disciples being puzzled by this parable of the weeds, even to the point of needing to ask Jesus what it means.

This leads us to the question of the day, "What does it mean?" What does this story of sowers; seeds, harvest and weeds tell us about God?

I would like to propose that this passage contains three of the great Matthean themes, which echo throughout Matthew's gospel. First, is the theme of God's judgment; second, the theme of the role of Christian discipleship; and third, the theme of God's grace. A grace that envelops the entire gospel.

The first theme is the theme of God's judgment. This is not a popular subject in today's culture. Yet, I ask you to stay with me for there are many blessing wrestling with this understanding. And the parable of the weeds provides us with many fascinating insights. After all, this is a passage describing some type of judgment.

However, this image of holy judgment is not based on what we may first expect. For this type of accountability is not based on our own human standards of right and wrong. But is found in the God of love, mercy and grace. A grace beyond our capacity to fathom. A seventy times seven type of forgiveness (Matthew 18:21-22).

Yet this grace beyond our capacity to fathom does not mean that anything goes. That there is no accountability for the decisions we make and the lives we seek to live. For this parable does include a time of weeding. A time of accountability.

To deny a time of accountability would not be a reading of this parable that attempts to remain true to the text. Further, to deny a time of accountability can reflect an understanding of cheap grace, which is very, very different from free grace. The free grace won for us all and for all peoples of the world by Jesus on that cross. "For freely, you have received, now freely give" (Matthew 10:8b).

Therefore, in the end, we are not left with easy, straight forward answers but rather we are left with a mysterious yet life enhancing tension. A life enhancing tension that forever moves as we deepen our personal, intimate relationship with God. Thus providing us with a basis for a dynamic relationship over a basis for eternal rules. And, (and this is key), at the same time it is not denying the necessity of human accountability. This accountability that adds meaning to life. For this judgment of the good, gracious, loving and merciful God, perfectly revealed, in and through Jesus, gives the gift of dignity to each person's life, since it provides importance to the decisions each person makes. It celebrates that the decisions we make do make a difference! And this gift of free will enables us to embrace and celebrate life!

The second theme is the role of Christian discipleship. For this parable is also clear in what it does not say about God's judgment. Simply stated, this passage indicates that the process of God's judgment, the process of "weeding" is not ours. For when Jesus is asked by his servants, "Do you want us to gather them?" (Meaning the weeds.) Jesus answers, "No, lest in gathering the weeds you root up the wheat along with them. Let them both grow together until the harvest; and at the harvest time I will tell the reapers: Gather the weeds first to be burned but gather the wheat into the barn."

Therefore, the importance of personal free will is maintained and also we realize that this judgment is the role of God. In this way, this parable echoes from an earlier place in the gospel of Matthew. Matthew 7:1-2, within the Sermon on the Mount, has Jesus teaching, "Judge not, that you be judged. For with the judgment you pronounce you will be judged, and the measure you give will be the measure you get."

Realizing this continuity in thought concerning the issue of judgment is helpful but it still does not adequately answer the original question concerning, "What this parable tells us about God."

It is here that we find that third great Mathean theme that envelops the entire gospel, the reality of God's grace.

But what does this grace look like? What does it feel like? Who is the one we trust in faith with the process of weeding? For this justice of God is surely beyond the justice we know. For this holy justice is God's and we know through Jesus that God is a God of salvation.

To shed light on what this saving justice might feel like I want to share an image. An image from a story you might have heard. I like to call it the "Starfish Dance".

It was a densely foggy day on the beach and an older man was making his daily walk along the beach. He walked rather slowly, somewhat bracing against the cool wind off the ocean. As he walked he saw something up ahead. The figure of a person, that seemed to be doing some type of strange dance in the morning midst. He continued his walk. Looking up on occasion to see more clearly what the morning dancer was doing.

As he got nearer, he realized that the figure he had seen was that of a young girl who was ever so carefully picking up a starfish that had washed ashore and then joyously skipping to the waters edge to carefully toss the starfish back into the water. Then the young girl would turn and continue her saving dance.

The older man finally came to where the young girl was and spoke to her. "Young girl," he said. "What are you doing? Don't you realize that there are hundreds of starfish that lay upon the beach and that what you are doing does not matter?"

The girl stopped her dance.

And she looked up and down the beach.

For as the morning sun had risen, the fog off the ocean had slowly lifted and only now could she see the many starfish that lay on either side of her on the beach.

The girl paused and looked down at the starfish that lay in her hands. And then a brilliant smile emerged on her face and a twinkle flickered in her eye and she looked at the man and said, "But it matters to this one." And she gently tossed the starfish back into the ocean and continued her saving starfish dance.

I think Faye Edgerton understood Jesus' teachings concerning the proper role of Christian discipleship and would have warmly smiled at the Starfish Dance. A short while ago, I was drawn to this little black and white book titled, <u>God</u>

<u>Speaks Navajo</u>.[1] I picked up the book and began to read it and as a result have begun to get to know Faye Edgerton.

Faye would feel God's lead to be a missionary to the Navajo people. A calling that she would dedicate nearly forty years of her life. But this somewhat frail looking woman of barely five feet would not be an ordinary missionary worker of her day. For missionaries of her day that served the Navajo people usually maintained their distance from these Native Americans. This distance was maintained through the way one dressed, where one lived and especially through one's language.

For the Navajo, who constituted the largest tribe of American Indians, numbering over one hundred thousand, spoke a native language called Dine bizaad. A language that was extremely difficult for English speaking missionaries to learn but also a language that maintained much of the Navajo people's enduring ethnic strength. The result of this inability to bridge that language barrier was the basic ineffectiveness of the Christian missionaries. That is, until Faye Edgerton came to the scene.

You see, Faye would take a different approach. An approach that meant she lived with the Navajo people, not in the comforts of the mission. It meant that she would get to know them and they know her and slowly she would grow to love them and they her.

There were many barriers that Faye would slowly cross. The final and most difficult barrier she would cross was to learn the Navajo language and eventually earn a new name. For Faye would earn the Navajo title, The-One-Who-Understands.

Faye describes the absolute necessity to learn Dine bizaad by simply describing the confusion surrounding the English word God. For the English word God pronounced by the Navajo sounded much like the Navajo word "gad", meaning

[1] Ethel Emily Wallis, *God Speaks Navajo*, (Harper and Row Publishers: New York, Evanston, London) 1968.

cedar tree. To some it sounded more like "gangi", meaning cow. Was this new god then a plant or animal they wondered?

When Christmas came and a tall cedar tree was decorated and set up in front of the church the Navajo concluded it must be a plant.

Such barriers as these were crossed when Faye learned the Navajo language. And the word of God was finally given to the Navajo people when Faye would translate the New Testament into Dine bizaad. When word circulated that she was undertaking this huge task most told her that she was wasting her time. They said that it could not be done and even if it were completed, the Navajo people would never accept it. But those critics were wrong.

For when this Bible translation was complete, it quickly sold out among the Navajo people. In fact, she would revise the New Testament translation seven times, as she better learned and understood the nuances of the Navajo language. Each of these revised translations would sell just as quickly until the Bible in the Navajo language would become the all-time best seller among the Navajo people. And the seeds of faith sowed through her faithful Christian witness would know no bounds among the Navajo people as they also received the gift of knowing and being known by the God of love, perfectly revealed through the Incarnate, Son Jesus Christ.

So, teacher, the parable of the weeds, "What does it mean?"

Jesus, the master teacher of us all, paused and looked down at the starfish that lay in his hands. And then a brilliant smile emerged on his face and a twinkle flickered in his eye and he gently tossed the starfish back into the sea and continued his saving starfish dance. That saving starfish dance that saves us all. Jesus' glorious saving starfish dance that saves us all…

May we, as we continue our own precious walks in faith, continue to grow in faith, love of God and service to neighbor, as we, like Faye Edgerton, each participate in God's wondrous and joyful saving starfish dance.

Amen

PERMISSION TO PRAY

Luke 11:1-13

He was praying in a certain place, and after he finished, one of
his disciples said to him,
"Lord, teach us to pray, as John taught his disciples."
He said to them, "When you pray say:

Father, hallowed be your name.
Your kingdom come.
Give us each day our daily bread.
And forgive us our sins,
for we ourselves forgive everyone indebted to us.
And do not bring to us the time of trial."

And he said to them, "Suppose one of you has a friend,
and you go to him, 'Friend, lend me three loaves of bread; for a
friend of mine has arrived, and I have nothing to set before him.'
And he answers from within, 'Do not bother me; the door has
already been locked, and my children are with me in bed; I
cannot get up and give you anything.' I tell you, even though he
will not get up and give him anything because he is his friend,
at least because of his persistence he will give him whatever he
needs.

"So I say to you, Ask and it will be given you: search, and you
will find; knock and the door will be opened for you.
For everyone who asks receives, and everyone who searches finds,
and for everyone who knocks, the door will be opened.

"Is there anyone among you who, if your child asks for a fish,
will give a snake instead of a fish?
Or if the child asks for an egg, will give a scorpion?

John Ruiz

"If you then,
who are evil know how to give good gifts to your children, how
much more will the heavenly Father give the Holy Spirit to those
who ask him!"

Meditation

(Traveling through this adventure called life: Fall 1996)

Pause with me for a moment to consider all the different kinds of breads that are used in churches throughout the world when celebrating the Lord's Supper. Consider for a moment the various languages that are speaking that incredible prayer that Jesus taught. Reflect for a moment at the many denominations within the Christian family that, while distinct, still profess a common love for God in Jesus Christ. This is a passage that transcends all barriers and unites Christians in prayer.

At the same time, an interesting challenge with this passage is to make it specific to our American context in the year 1996. To do this I decided to use a form of mass media that has been mastered in our society. It is also one of my favorite restaurants, McDonalds.

A McDonald's commercial from our recent past showed a young father and all the things that require his energies during the day. You see him washing the car, at work, playing with his kids and at various additional responsibilities. Finally, you see him leaning against his station wagon eating a double Big Mac. In fact, that is the purpose of the commercial. It advertises a double Big Mac because this man is so busy that just a regular Big Mac won't satisfy his hunger. The whole deluxe sandwich series builds on this basic idea.

My purpose is not to advertise McDonald's sandwiches. But rather it is to uplift a common reality that we know and live. We all know what it is like to have countless responsibilities and activities pull on our time and energy.

A recent Newsweek article reports that work time is up and leisure time is down. And this runs across age, sex, race and economic barriers. We are a busy people, running busy lives and trying for all we are worth to juggle all of the responsibilities and obligations we have.

There are work obligations that no longer end at forty hours a week but all too frequently bleed over to other times. Many times these obligations even enter into our homes with telephones, answering services and lap top computers.

This is no wonder. We are a society that really does live out the phrase, "The early bird gets the worm." And we have to and we do work hard to provide for ourselves and for our loved ones.

Our society seems to disdain idle time. One must rush it seems at times for the sole purpose of rushing. And this is not a guy thing or a female thing or even a parent thing.

I tutored children for two years while going to seminary and it was not uncommon for fifth or sixth graders to have planner pads that inform them of all the activities and obligations that they have on a given day. The day of a common family dinner is the exception for many of today's families. This is the result of the family attempting to juggle four or five planner pad schedules.

Even Sundays do not provide a sense of reprieve. Many youth practices and games now fall on Sundays, even at times previously designed for Sunday worship. Further, we need only drive down the street to find countless persons who have to be at work on Sunday, at restaurants, gas stations, and department stores. The list is full of places that are open with persons working on a Sunday and even during Sunday worship times.

In the midst of this hectic pace the question becomes, "How does this passage relate?" What can the words of Jesus teaching the disciples to pray, the prayer we know as the Lord's Prayer, say in our day? What specific blessing can this prayer have for our mile a minute American culture? What fresh insights can we draw from this timeless prayer?

I want to propose one fresh insight, just one insight, but the gifts known from this one precious insight can truly be life transforming. Simply stated, Jesus teaching the disciples to pray means we have permission to pray.

Notice the gift is the permission to pray, not the obligation or duty to pray. We have the permission to pray, to talk to God, to listen to God's guidance, to be embraced by God's love.

Realize the utter freedom of this gift! For this means we have permission to hold hands with loved ones and bow our head in prayer before a family meal.

We have permission to pause during our fifteen minute, work break and quietly talk with God.

We have permission to walk through the woods during our lunch hour and be enveloped by God's wondrous creation.

We have permission to lay our deepest worries, fears and anxieties into the arms of the God of hope when tragedy strikes or the doctor gives us difficult or terrible news that we do not know how to bear.

We have permission to pray, through listening to music, or singing our favorite hymn as we drive to work, transport kids to practice or race our way to the grocery store.

We have permission to start our day with a quiet cup of coffee and a moment of silence with God.

We have permission to say nightly prayers with our children and gently kiss them, "God Bless You", as we tuck them into bed.

We have permission to pray and we have permission to seek that place we have known to be holy. Maybe it is a sanctuary, a quiet place in the woods, a cup of coffee while sitting on the porch on an autumn morning, entering the chapel of a church alone and pausing, in a living room with a loved one or friend, or in a rocking chair while holding a little one. We have permission to pray.

Further, this permission is ours now! For if we wait for our work place, or our boss, or our culture in general to give us permission to pray then we will be waiting a long, long time.

Finally, this permission to pray and the freedom known in this gift does not come from a pastor or from a church but this permission to pray and the resultant freedom one knows comes from Jesus who teaches the disciples to pray.

This passage is from the gospel of Luke, and prayer is a central theme throughout Luke's gospel. This is the fifth time within the first eleven chapters of this gospel that we are told of Jesus praying.

Luke 3:21-22, at Jesus' baptism reads, "When all people were being baptized, Jesus was baptized too. And as he was praying, heaven was opened and the Holy Spirit descended on him in bodily form like a dove. And a voice came from heaven: 'You are my Son, whom I love; with you I am well pleased.'"

Luke 6:12-13, when Jesus calls the twelve apostles. "One of those days Jesus went out on a mountainside to pray, and spent the night praying to God. When morning came, he called his disciples to him and chose twelve of them, whom he designated apostles."

Luke 9:18 and Peter's confession of Christ. When Peter answers Jesus' question, "Who do you say that I am?" by responding, "The Christ of God." This passage begins in verse 18, "Once when Jesus was praying in private and his disciples were with him, he asked them, 'Who do the crowds say that I am?'"

Finally, Luke 9:29 and the transfiguration of Jesus reads, "As he was praying the appearance of his face changed and his clothes became as bright as a flash of lightening."

Jesus prayed and was filled with God's spirit. He received guidance and strength. His will became God's will.

Jesus praying gives us permission to do likewise. This is permission to stop, to reflect, to commune with God. To be filled with the Holy Spirit. To dream dreams. To give away and surrender our deepest worries, fears, and tragedies, to receive guidance, to be at peace.

48

We have permission to pray. And we have the model of Jesus who stopped and prayed and called God, Father, and taught us to do likewise.

We have permission to pray. Further, we have the assurance of a loving and faithful God who gives us the gifts of the Holy Spirit. The theologian Fred Craddock writes in his commentary, "The gift of the Holy Spirit is central in Luke for understanding both Jesus (Luke 3:21) and the church (Luke 24:49; Acts 1:4,5; 2:38). The Holy Spirit leads and empowers Jesus, and when the Holy Spirit comes to Jesus' followers (Acts 1:8) they will be led and empowered to continue what Jesus began to do and to teach before he was received up. Without the Holy Spirit there was not, there is not, a church."[1]

John Wesley expressed this understanding concerning the essential aspect of the gift of prayer for the Christian and the guidance that comes from the Holy Spirit. Wesley wrote this short letter to a lay pastor serving a small parish who complained that he was too busy to find time for prayer and reflection. Wesley sent this reply, "O begin! Fix some time each day for prayer and scripture. Do it; whether you like it or no. It is for your life! Else you be a trifler all your days."[2]

We have permission to pray.

Amen

[1] Fred B. Craddock, *Luke: Interpretation A Bible Commentary for Teaching and Preaching*, (John Knox Press: Louisville) 1990, p. 154.
[2] John Wesley wrote this short letter. Prof. Paul Chilcote read it during the class, DS 380 United Methodism I, in the fall quarter of 1995 at the Methodist Theological School in Ohio.

THE ART OF STEERING

Luke 24:13-35

Now on that same day two of them were going to a village called Emmaus, about seven miles from Jerusalem. They were talking with each other about everything that had happened.

As they talked and discussed these things with each other, Jesus himself came up and walked along with them; but they were kept from recognizing him.

He asked them,
"What are you discussing together as you walk along?"

They stood still, their faces downcast.
One of them, named Cleopas, asked him,
"Are you only a visitor in Jerusalem and do not know the things that have happened there in these days?"

"What things?" he asked.

"About Jesus of Nazareth," they replied.
"He was a prophet, powerful in word and deed before God and all the people. The chief priests and our rulers handed him over to be sentenced to death, and they crucified him; but we had hoped that he was the one who was going to redeem Israel. And what is more, it is the third day since this took place. In addition, some of our women amazed us. They went to the tomb
early this morning but didn't find his body.
They came and told us that they had seen a vision of angels, who said he was alive.
Then some of our companions went to the tomb and found it just as the Women had said, but him they did not see."

He said to them,
"How foolish you are, and how slow of heart to believe all that
the prophets have spoken! Did not the Christ have to suffer these
things and then enter his glory?" And beginning with Moses and
all the Prophets, he explained to them what was said in all the
scriptures concerning himself."

As they approached the village to which they were going, Jesus
acted as if he were going farther. But they urged him strongly,
"Stay with us, for it is nearly evening; the day is almost over."
So he went to stay with them.

When he was at the table with them,
He took bread, gave thanks, broke it and began to give it to
them.
Then their eyes were opened and they recognized him, and he
disappeared from their sight.

They asked each other,
"Were not our hearts burning within us while he talked with us
on the road and opened the scriptures to us?"

They got up and returned at once to Jerusalem.
There they found the eleven and those with them, assembled
together
And saying, "It is true! The Lord has risen and has appeared to
Simon."
Then they told what had happened on the way, and how Jesus
was recognized
by them when he broke the bread.

Meditation

(Traveling through this adventure called life: Spring 1997)

In the meditation, *The Starfish Dance*, we met Faye Edgerton a woman who faithfully represented the gospel of Jesus Christ to the Navajo people by living within the Navajo community, learning the Navajo language and translating the New Testament into the Navajo language. The vision of the meditation was to uplift the idea and challenge the development of relationships of ministering with each other. Especially with the poor and not fostering relationships of ministering to each other and to the poor. For the first relationship is based upon mutual giving and dignity. While the later can develop into one-way giving which can strip a person or people of their dignity.

As I was preparing this meditation, my mind reflected back to the Starfish Dance, this scripture text of Jesus on the Emmaus road, and this meditation titled "The Art of Steering". For the Art of Steering builds upon our joining Jesus' saving starfish dance in which we develop the eyes to see and the awareness to notice the wondrous acts of God in our midst.

Noticing the wondrous acts of God in our midst can be a difficult thing, especially in the hectic, never stop pace of many of our lives. When I arrived and began to serve at Church of the Messiah, in Westerville, Ohio a number of people described this adventure as a rushing river. A river that rushes whether one wants it to or not. A river that can roar and sweep one up into a state of confusion, disorientation, and in some cases, mindless activity solely for the sake of keeping busy.

Perhaps some of us can identify with this picture for we too live lives that can be hectic, where currents can seem to disorient us, and where the barrage of constant activity can make it difficult to stop and think and focus in on what is most important. To see the face of God in our lives. And it is here that the Art of Steering can provide us a boat by which we can steer life's adventures and rejoice in the beauty of life that God has given us.

This passage gives us a key. For within this passage we meet two persons who had recently experienced a flurry of activity that had left them confused, disoriented and in despair. And it is here that a risen Savior meets them on the road, talks with them, and stands near them. But they do not realize this moment in their lives for the scripture tells us that, "They stood still, their eyes downcast."

God, through Christ, was meeting them as God meets us, but they never noticed because their eyes were downcast. Their eyes were not focused on God, nor were they looking for a risen Lord. For their eyes were downcast and focused on the flurry of the previous days activity.

It is here that the Art of Steering begins, for the Art of Steering means maintaining one's vision, and being faithful in the moment, thus allowing God to enable us to soar!

A few weeks ago the Young Adults groups called YACHT clubs (Young Adult Christians Hanging Together) headed to the Ronal MacDonald's House to provide those persons staying there with a hot meal and praise music. We arrived at the house, served the meal and began to settle around the tables so we could enjoy sloppy Joes and share in conversation and music. Many persons from both groups wanted to sing so we gave out songbooks and someone began to lead us in music.

I was mingling with our new friends. First, I talked with a spunky 4th grade girl, who was being treated with chemotherapy for ovarian cancer, and her mother. Their spirits were good. The young girl only had a few more treatments and the therapy seemed to be working. The mother seemed to enjoy the music and the attention that many in the group were giving to her daughter.

I decided to continue to another table. I had noticed that every table had more than one person except one. At this table sat a woman, alone, with a note pad. She was an unassuming woman wearing black-framed glasses and had tattoos on her arms. I approached the table, said "Hi" and cautiously asked how things were going. She looked up, gave a sigh and said, "Okay, I am just trying to write a letter to the birth mother of Noah and it's really hard to know what to say." Intrigued and a little startled I asked if I could sit down and hear more about Noah.

I sat down and Sherri began to tell me that she and her husband had adopted a special needs infant named Noah and she had been there nine days because Noah had been born with water on the brain. She hoped they would be able to go home tomorrow. Amazed I expressed what a wonderful thing she was doing and how difficult it must have been to be there all this time. To which she amazed me all the more for she began to talk not of herself but of her husband and family. You see, Noah was the seventh special needs child she and her husband had adopted. And her thoughts were more on concerns for them.

She explained how her husband and the oldest boy, Steve, had been getting along okay but she missed them. She talked proudly of Steve's successes over the past years and how he came to them as a youth and was very withdrawn but now he was out-going and helped greatly with his brothers and sisters. She talked excitedly of their future because they had purchased a house in South Carolina with thirteen rooms, all on one floor, which would make managing their home much easier since many of the children had trouble getting around and since she expected they would adopt three special needs siblings at summer's end and needed more room. She talked of her faith and was impressed at the sign language some of the young adults were doing with the music. Inspired I said goodbye to Sherri, realizing we had come to give to them and had received greatly in return.

For relationships of ministering with each other are based upon mutual giving and dignity and the Art of Steering means maintaining one's vision. How easy it would have been to walk right by this woman of faith and miss seeing the face of Christ in her witness.

Next week this church will embark on an incredible journey as the youth of the church, with the help of many adults and this entire church, are hosts to 11 youth and 11 adults from Puerto Rico for a time of mission. The groups will help build a house in the greater Columbus area through Habitat for Humanity, work at Southside Settlement Camp and in various modes throughout Westerville. We will spend time together in fellowship and sharing of our talents and faith.

It is living out a relationship based upon mutual giving and dignity. The question arises, as it always does in our frantic lives, "Will we maintain our vision to see the face of Christ in our guests faithful witness by being present in the moment thus allowing God to enable us to soar?"

In mid-May we had our UMYF spring retreat. On Saturday we began our day with a morning devotion. The group was gathered in a semi-circle around the campfire pit. We sang, read scripture, had a meditation spoken and moments of reflection. We were sitting as a group listening to what would happen next. I was sitting towards the back of the group as someone was describing the weekend's art project when I felt eyes on me. You know the feeling you get when someone is looking at you. No one was behind me and something made me look up to see a gorgeous hawk soaring directly above the group. Many of the youth followed my lead and also looked up to see this incredible sight. A couple even whispered, "Doesn't it seem like God might be getting our attention."

The Art of Steering means maintaining one's vision so we can notice God's mighty acts in our lives and being faithful in the moment thus allowing God to enable us to soar.

It means recognizing how God has embraced us through the Angels we have known. Some who may now be in heaven, but upon whose shoulders we stand. Who seemingly teach our red heads to bat and even now continue to teach us to pray. Who smile with pride and cheer our faithfulness (Hebrews 12:1).

It means listening to the prayers of another. I am still, at times, overcome by the faithfulness I have experienced on hospital visits over the past few years. I usually finish a visit by holding hands and with a prayer, where everyone gathered has the opportunity to speak. Then we close with the Lord's Prayer. There are times when I visit and the person I am visiting is very sick. During these times I hold hands and pray out loud for them. On more than one occasion, while praying the Lord's Prayer, I have been stunned to hear someone who I was not even sure knew I was there join me in prayer.

The Art of Steering means recognizing the beauty of friendships, the love of a sister, the daily courage of a brother, the hope and steadfast faith given from a mother or father. It means stopping to savor the joy given in one's children, marveling at how they grow. It means cherishing those relationships that last a lifetime.

It means stopping to take the time to talk with another. Have you ever noticed that those persons who seem to walk the tallest in their faithfulness always seem to have time to sit and share a cup of coffee or a banana and quiet conversation? Just think how many times we hear of Jesus sitting and talking with those around him, even with the sinners, tax collectors and outcasts of his day.

At conference Bishop Minor shared a working of the church in Russia that is built upon this foundation of mutual sharing and dignity.[1] He told of an epidemic his country is experiencing with the rise of poverty and the growth of street children. It is estimated that there are now 50,000 street children in Moscow alone. The government's response to this crisis has been to develop "Housing Facilities" though they look much more like detention facilities. In fact, he related that children have broken out of these "housing facilities".

The church, however, has chosen a different response. The church has developed "havens" where one can come to shower, have something to eat and a place to sleep. It is hoped that the children will choose to stay but there is always the choice. A choice they otherwise would not have. A choice he admits can be heartbreaking when some choose to leave.

However, it is a choice built upon God's love. For it is a choice built upon the dignity one enjoys when one is given their God-given right to choose. Bishop Minor described this for a definition of evangelism. The giving of a choice concerning God in Christ both to those persons we know and are in the fold and also to those persons we do not know and may not know the love of God.

The Art of Steering means seeing God active in the sacraments as their eyes were opened with the breaking of the bread or the sharing of Christian baptism. It means feeding upon the scriptures as Jesus opened the scriptures to them and to us. It means taking the permission we all have to commune with God in prayer. It means realizing life's joys are abundant for we live our lives saved within the mighty acts of God's grace perfectly revealed through the Son, Jesus Christ and not through the works of our own actions. It means maintaining one's vision and being faithful in the moment thus allowing God to enable us to soar.

In conclusion, I end with this old story I first encountered quite some time ago and has been passed down about a man

[1] Bishop Minor shared messages at the West Ohio Annual Conference of the United Methodist Church in June 1996.

who was hiking in the hills near his home one day and found a strange looking egg.[2] This man happened to own a poultry farm so he placed this strange looking egg in the incubator to be hatched with the other eggs. In time, the strange looking egg produced a strange looking bird.

And so it was that even though it had a peculiar air about it and was obviously out of place among the other birds, the farmer decided that he would raise the bird like a chicken since chickens were all he ever raised. Soon, because all this bird ever saw were chickens, because all he was ever given to eat was chicken feed, because day in and day out he was treated like a chicken, because the only name he was ever called was "chicken", this bird began to act like a chicken. He lost his peculiar air and no longer seemed so out of place.

One day a visitor came to the farm, and while he was walking through the yard, he saw this strange looking bird. He walked up to the farmer and asked him why he had an eagle living among his chickens.

The farmer replied, "He may look like an eagle, but I has raised him to be a chicken. He lives among the chickens. He eats like a chicken. The only life he knows is the life of a chicken. So a chicken is all he will ever be."

The visitor said, "You can not callously tamper with the soul of God's creation. God has placed within the bird the seeds of greatness, and you have confined it to the barnyard. However, no creature God has intended to fly in lofty places is beyond redemption, no matter how long it has been in the barnyard. This bird may have the habits of a chicken, but deep down within, where your environment can't reach, God has placed the heart and soul of an eagle."

The visitor lifted the eagle and said, "God did not create you to be a chicken. God created you to be an eagle; so stretch forth your wings and fly." The eagle took off from the visitor's

[2] William D. Watley, *Sermons From the Black Pulpit*, (Judson Press, Valley Forge) 1984, p. 104-106.

hand. But as it was ascending, the farmer threw some chicken feed on the ground, and the eagle flew right back down to the ground and started eating the feed. The farmer looked at the visitor and said, "I told you he was nothing but a chicken."

At this point the visitor took the eagle and climbed to the top of the barn where the eagle could see more of the countryside and behold that there was a world beyond the barnyard. He told the eagle a second time, "God did not create you to be a chicken but an eagle; so stretch forth your wings and fly."

Again the bird took off, ascending. Again, the farmer threw feed on the ground, and again the eagle flew down to the ground. The farmer once again turned to the visitor and said, "I told you that he was nothing but a chicken."

But refusing to give up, the visitor asked the farmer if he could try one more time. Early the next morning, while it was still yet dark, the visitor placed the eagle under his arm and started climbing up a high mountain. As he approached the summit, the sun was beginning to break the darkness of the eastern horizon.

The visitor pointed the eagle toward the rising sun, the risen Son who saves us ALL!, and said a third time, "You were not created to be a chicken but an eagle, so stretch forth your wings and fly!"

The rays of that blessed risen Savior struck the piercing gleam in the eagle's eye. His body began to tremble with pulsating energy, and with one great leap, on outstretched wings, the eagle flew away toward the dawning of a new day, not looking back and not looking down, only toward the greatness God intended.

May God bless us all as we seek to maintain our vision and be faithful in the moment thus allowing God to enable us to soar like an eagle, all for the glory of God.

Amen

A SAILOR'S GRIP

Acts 8: 1b-6

That day a severe persecution began against the church in Jerusalem, and all except the apostles were scattered throughout the countryside of Judea and Samaria. Devout men buried Stephen and made loud lamentations over him.
But Saul was ravaging the church by entering house after house; dragging off both men and women, he committed them to prison.

Now those who were scattered went from place to place, proclaiming the word.
Philip went down to the city of Samaria and proclaimed the Messiah to them.
The crowds with one accord listened eagerly to what was said by Philip hearing and seeing the signs he did.

Acts 9: 1-4

Meanwhile Saul, still breathing threats and murder against the disciples of the Lord, went to the high priest and asked him for letters to the synagogue at Damascus, so that if he found any who belonged to the Way, men or women, he might bring them bound to Jerusalem.

Now as he was going along and approaching Damascus, suddenly a light from heaven flashed around him. He fell to the ground and heard a voice saying to him, "Saul, Saul, why do you persecute me?"

Luke 18: 35-43

As he approached Jericho, a blind man was sitting by the roadside begging.

When he heard the crowds going by, he asked what was
happening.
They told him, "Jesus of Nazareth is passing by."

Then he shouted,
"Jesus, Son of David, have mercy on me!"

Those who were in front sternly ordered him to be quiet; but he
shouted even more loudly,
"Son of David, have mercy on me!"

Jesus stood still and ordered the man to be brought to him; and
when he came near he asked him, "What do you want me to do
for you?"

He said,
"Lord, let me see again."

Jesus said to him,
"Receive your sight; your faith has saved you."

Immediately he regained his sight and followed him
glorifying God; and all the people, when they saw it,
praised God.

Meditation

(Traveling through this adventure called life: Fall 1998)

This past summer I had the privilege of hearing Bishop Peter Storey speak on two occasions.[1] Bishop Storey is a Methodist Bishop in South Africa. For many years he has been a voice for those who had no voice in his country. In other words, he was someone who spoke out against Apartheid, long before it was the popular thing to do. Apartheid being a political system that systematically kept people in place. Simply because of one's color one would be regulated to only certain opportunities within that country. Bishop Storey preached against Apartheid because he understood it to be incongruent with the gospel of Jesus Christ. He understood from the gospel of Jesus Christ that all persons are precious in the sight of God. That all persons regardless of their color, if they are male or female, if they talk or look different, that all persons are made in the image of God and therefore are precious. And because they are precious, all persons must have the opportunity to pursue the dreams that God has given them.

Therefore, Bishop Storey felt he must speak out against Apartheid. When he first stood up for those in his country who had no voice, he was met with criticism, anger and many times he was an outcast (even among his clergy peers). However, he continued to stand up for those who can't and was part of awakening his country, and in a way, the world, to more seriously consider Jesus' teaching within the treatment of all our neighbors. Until today, we can celebrate that Apartheid is a thing of the past in South Africa.

When Bishop Storey spoke he said many things, and one of the things that has stayed with me the most is an image he gave us. It is an image I would like to share with you. It

[1] Bishop Storey shared messages at the Wisconsin Annual Conference of the United Methodist Church in June 1998.

is the image of a sailor's grip, that for him is a symbol of our relationship with the God of love and grace.

A sailor's grip. This image can be an illustration for these scripture passages.

A sailor's grip, two hands clutching each other, forming a tight bond signifies whenever a person says, "yes" to God. Whenever a person says, "yes" to God there is a moment of what is called justifying grace and a covenantal bond is formed between God and that person.

"Yes, God, I will grab hold of your loving hand that continually reaches our for me and all persons everywhere. I will grab hold and hang on during all of life's adventures. The good times and the bad."

This "yes" moment can happen in countless ways, perhaps during an individual quiet moment, or a Confirmation, perhaps when one takes Communion or at a Baptism. Perhaps it is a dramatic moment that stays with a person for a lifetime or one of many little moments that can occur everyday, or many times a day, as one says "yes" to God in his or her own way. It can be a dinnertime or nighttime prayer, through a song. These "yes' experiences can occur in countless ways.

Just like that blind beggar by the side of the road who calls out to Jesus even when others tell him to be quiet. But he remains committed in faith and keeps calling out and as a result is healed by God in a very special way and is able to see God in new ways as a result. Just like those early Christians who were persecuted. Forced to leave their livelihoods and homes, some put into prison, others like Stephen killed (Acts 6:8-8:a). Who remained faithful, who kept hanging on in the sailor's grip and telling others of the love of God known in Jesus Christ.

However, this is only part of the story because the sailor's grip has two hands bonding together. One represents our hand and the other represents God's. Therefore, we know that even when times are toughest, God hangs onto us. In other words, even when we think we can't hang on any longer, God hangs onto us. We see this in Philip. Philip, a disciple of Jesus Christ, who goes into Samaria during a time of persecution and proclaims the good news of Christ. Thus Philip brings many persons to know God in Christ and also reassures all those who have scattered that God is still there.

"Look, there is one of his disciples right over there who continues to know God and speaks of God's blessings when times look the bleakest!" Yes, God remains with us holding onto us when things might look the bleakest.

However, once again this is only part of the story. For there is also Saul. Saul who had persecuted the Christians. Saul who was traveling to Damascus in his continuing attempts to wipe out all of Christianity. How easy it would have been to write Saul off. He is too far-gone! He has sinned too much. How easy it would have been for God to have decided that Saul is unredeemable, a permanent outcast, just like we might say to someone we believe has wronged us.

Only that is not the way God is. No, the sailor's grip means God is always reaching out. Reaching out for Saul. Reaching out for us. Reaching out for all peoples. You see, when others may have given up on us, when we might have given up on ourselves, God in Christ hasn't given up. Yes, even when no one else believes in us, God still believes in us, and God still reaches out to us. Just like with Saul on that Damascus road. Saul, who we know better as Paul. Who as Paul would become one of the most significant preachers of the gospel of Jesus Christ that the world has ever known. For God continues to reach out for us wanting to form that sailor's grip.

However, this is still not the end of the story. For there are times when we might actually have lost our grip. When we feel like Peter when he stepped out of that boat and was sinking in the stormy waters (Matthew 14:22-36). And somehow we have in our confusion or lack of faith, lost our grip. Well, what happens when one person lets go in the sailor's grip?

There is still one hand holding on. For even when we slip and let go, God's hand continues to hold steady. For even when we can't, God can!

That is why sailors developed the sailor's grip in the first place. So that when they were out at sea and a storm arose, this grip provided greater safety. It is much stronger than a handgrip. Further, if during the confusion of the storm one person's hand would slip and they may cast overboard, the other sailor's grip would continue to hold on and keep them safely on board.

A sailor's grip. God in Jesus Christ forming a sailor's grip with us. Praise God!

Amen

UNITED WE PRESS
TOWARDS THE GOAL

Philippians 3:4b-14

*If anyone else has reason to be confident in the flesh I have more:
circumcised on the eighth day, a member of the people of Israel,
of the tribe of Benjamin, a Hebrew born of Hebrews; as to the
law, a Pharisee; as to zeal, a persecutor of the church; as to
righteousness under the law, blameless.*

*Yet whatever gains I had, these I have come to regard as loss
because of Christ.
More than that, I regard everything as loss because of the
surpassing value of knowing Christ Jesus my Lord.*

*For this sake I have suffered the loss of all things, and I regard
them as rubbish, in order that they may gain Christ and be
found in him, not having a righteousness of my own that comes
from the law, but one that comes from faith in Christ, and the
righteousness from God based on faith.*

*I want to know Christ and the power of his resurrection and the
sharing of his sufferings by becoming like him in his death, if
somehow I may attain the resurrection from the dead.*

*Not that I have already obtained this or have already reached the
goal; but I press on to make it my own, because Christ Jesus has
made me his own.
Beloved, I do not consider that I have made it my own; but this
one thing I do: forgetting what lies behind and straining forward
to what lies ahead.*

*I press toward the goal
for the prize of the heavenly call of God in Jesus Christ.*

John Ruiz

Meditation

(Traveling through this adventure called life: Fall 1999)

In this meditation I am going to focus on three thoughts that can arise from this passage. The first thought comes from verse 9 where it reads, "Not having a righteousness of my own that comes form the law, but one that comes from faith in Christ, the righteousness from God based on faith."

In this way, the apostle Paul is focusing not on the things that divide but rather on the things that unite. And for those residing within the Christian community the foundation of this unity is Christ.

The theologian Fred Craddock states the issue clearly. "The issue was not the adequacy of the grace of God to make righteous those who trust in his grace."[1] Not human effort or achievement.

A second thought that can be found throughout the letter Philippians (a letter Paul writes to the church at Philippi while in jail) involves Paul working with and redefining the nature of suffering. Both the suffering he might have experienced for his faith in Christ as well as that experienced by the church.

Paul seems to almost make illusions to joining Christ in His suffering. And it is important to remember that God does not create our suffering. However, God can help us endure our suffering with courage and optimism. And even help us to use our suffering to serve others in their times and places of loss and pain.

There are many examples of these types of situations and groups, grief counselors, Aids workers and various addiction groups, to name a few. In this way, perhaps our embracing our own experiences of suffering may free us to do this more.

---

[1] Fred B. Craddock, *Philippians: Interpretation A Bible Commentary for Teaching and Preaching*, (John Knox Press: Atlanta) 1985, p. 56.

74

To summarize this thought I turn once again to Fred Craddock when he writes, "Christ's suffering enabled Paul to interpret his own, and his own suffering enabled him to interpret Christ's."[2]

And finally, a third point is the image of pressing on towards the goal from verses 12-14. First, Paul unites the community, and us as well, in a "righteousness from God based on faith" and then he talks about his (and in turn our) pressing on towards the goal.

In hard times we press on. In good times we press on. Through times of sorrow we press on. In moments of great rejoicing we press on. United in faith we press on…

Amen

[2] Ibid, p. 60-61.

A MESSAGE FROM PAUL

Philippians 1:1-14

Paul and Timothy, servants of Christ Jesus, to all the saints in Christ Jesus who are in Philippi, with the bishops and deacons: grace to you and peace from God our Father and the Lord Jesus Christ.

I thank my God every time I remember you, constantly praying with you in every one of my prayers for all of you, because of your sharing in the gospel from the first day until now. I am confident of this, that the one who began a good work among you will bring it to completion by the day of Jesus Christ. It is right for me to think this way about all of you, because you hold me in your heart, for all or you share in God's grace with me, both in my imprisonment and in the compassion of Jesus Christ. And this is my prayer, that your love may overflow more and more with knowledge and full insight to help you to determine what is best, so that in the day of Christ you may be pure and blameless, having produced the harvest of righteousness that comes through Jesus Christ for the glory and praise of God.

I want you to know, beloved, that what happened to me has actually helped to spread the gospel, so that it has become known throughout the whole imperial guard and to everyone else that my imprisonment is for Christ; and most of the brothers and sisters, having been made confident in the Lord by my imprisonment, dare to speak the word with greater boldness and without fear.

Philippians 1:21-30

For to me, living in Christ and dying is gain.
If I am to live in the flesh, that means fruitful labor for me; and I do not know which I prefer. I am hard pressed between the two: my desire to depart and be with Christ, for that is far

better, but to remain in the flesh is more necessary for you. Since I am convinced of this, I know I will remain and continue with all of you for your progress and joy in faith, so that I may share abundantly in your boasting in Christ Jesus when I come to you again.

Only, live your life in a manner worthy of the gospel of Christ, so that whether I come and see you or am absent and hear about you, I will know that you are standing from in one spirit, striving side by side with one mind for the faith of the gospel, and are in no way intimidated by your opponents. For them this is evidence of their destruction, but of your salvation.

And this is God's doing.
For he has graciously granted you the privilege not only of believing in Christ, but of suffering for him as well- since you are having the same struggle that you saw I had and now hear that I still have.

Meditation

(Traveling through this adventure called life: Fall 1999)

In this meditation we will be looking at two passages from Paul's letter to the church at Philippi. Paul is in prison while writing this letter (though the exact location of the jail is debated among Biblical scholars.) So from Paul's jail cell he composes these words to a church he helped to start. As we look at the beginning of this letter I invite you to ask yourself, "What is the tone of the letter?" "How has Paul perceived the church and those who make up the church in the past?" And finally, "What might Paul's purpose for this letter be?"

As we noted, these two passages are part of a letter written to the church at Philippi. Paul's missionary style was to establish congregations in major urban centers and then after a time move on. So a letter would be the next best thing to being there. The letter would be read orally to the Christian assembly. Further, the letters functioned to create a kind of personal presence with the readers (hearers) and also functioned as an official, authoritative presence as though Paul was there himself. Thus the Philippians letter would create what Fred Craddock calls "Intimate distance."[1]

To my reading, the tone of this letter begins in a warm way. Paul seems to have genuinely fond feelings for the church. And this letter is giving the church and its members encouragement.

It also appears that Paul perceives the church in a very positive way. Part of verse 5 reads, "sharing in ministry in both imprisonment and in the defense and confirmation of the gospel." (Though at the same time we might have recognized the beginning of an illusion to some problems emerging within the community that we will look at in a later meditation.)

[1] Fred Craddock, *Philippians: Interpretation A Bible Commentary for Teaching and Preaching*, (John Knox Press: Atlanta) 1985, p. 1-7.

John Ruiz

Finally, Paul's purpose for writing this letter is to give encouragement. Encouragement in spreading the gospel of Jesus Christ at all times, even in the midst of difficult situations.

Paul even defines the function of his imprisonment in a positive way since Paul's imprisonment has helped spread the gospel. First, the gospel of Christ has spread among the imperial guard and Paul's faithfulness has also emboldened others thus making them less fearful in sharing the gospel.

In this way, Paul's experience is similar to that of the Philippi church who has experienced suffering for their faith in Christ. Therefore, Paul is encouraging and calling the church to continue to be God's people in their place and time. To continue being partners in the gospel.

A little while later Paul introduces something we looked at in the previous meditation *United We Press Towards the Goal*. Paul changes our understanding of suffering. Remembering that God doesn't create our suffering. However, God can help us endure our suffering with courage and optimism. And even help us use our suffering to serve others in their times and places of loss and pain. Redefining the nature of suffering is very important for Paul to do when we recognize that both Paul's and also the church's reality has not been easy since their acceptance of Christ. Yet even within their hardships there remains joy, optimism and courage because of Christ.

This idea is stated very clearly in 1:29-30, "For he has graciously granted you the privilege not only of believing in Christ but of suffering for him as well-since you are having the same struggle that you saw I had and now hear I have."

It was in this light and remembering, Paul wrote this letter while in prison, that I was drawn to an article I read awhile back, found in the book Finding God in Unexpected Places written by Philip Yancey titled, "The Church Behind Bars."[2]

[2] Philip Yancey, *Finding God in Unexpected Places*, (Servant Publications: Ann Arbor, Michigan) 1997, p. 189-203.

Yancey writes a good friend, Ron Nikkel, invited me to visit some Christians in the prisons of Chile and Peru. South American jails, I knew, would provide an extreme test of faith for anyone. Although conditions have improved now, at the time Chile was viewed as one of the world's worst human rights violators. And Peruvian jails also made news headlines.

What does a "church" look like among lumpen people such as these: fenced in, ill-fed, vulnerable to sexual assaults, sentenced to life of misery among murderers, thieves, rapist, and drug dealers? Can the hope of the Christian message survive those conditions? I decided to find out.

I am sitting in the midst of a church service with a distinctly Latin and Pentecostal flavor. On the platform, a "band" consisting of eighteen guitarists, one accordionist, and two men wielding homemade brass tambourines is leading a rousing rendition of a folksy song called "The Banquet of the Lord."

The congregation, 150 strong, lustily joins in. Some people raise their hands above their heads. Some seem to be competing in a highest decibel contest. A few hug their neighbors. The meeting room is overflowing, and extra faces are peering in all the windows.

Except for a few visual reminders, I could easily forget that we are meeting in one of the largest prisons in Chile. I look around at the congregation: all men, wearing a ragtag assortment of handed-down street clothes. A shocking number of their faces are marked with scars.

After singing a Canadian guest, conspicuous in a white shirt and tie, comes to the platform. The prison chaplain informs the crowd that this man, Ron Nikkel, has visited prisons in more than fifty countries. The organization he directs, Prison Fellowship International, brings the message of Christ to prisoners and works with governments on improving prison condition. A dozen inmates yell a loud "Amen!"

"I bring you greetings from your brothers and sisters in Christ in prisons around the world," Ron begins, pausing for the translation into Spanish. He is a broad-shouldered man of moderate height, with a freckled face that gives a youthful look. His soft voice must compete with noise flowing in from the outside- guards blowing whistles, inmates playing basketball in the exercise yard, music blaring from cell blocks.

"I bring you greeting especially from Pascal, who lives in Africa, in a country called Madagascar. Pascal trained as a scientist and took pride in his atheism. One day he was arrested for participating in a strike. He was thrown into a prison designed for 800 men, but now crowded with 2,500 men. They sat elbow to elbow on bare boards, most of them dressed in rags and covered with lice. You can imagine the situation there." The Chilean inmates, who have been listening alertly, groan aloud with sympathy.

"Pascal had only one book available in prison- a Bible provided by his family. He read it daily, and despite his atheistic beliefs he began to pray. He found that science could not help him in prison." (Loud laughter.) "By the end of three months, Pascal was leading a Bible study every night in the crowded room."

"Much to his surprise, Pascal was released after three months. Someone in the government had a change in heart. But here is the amazing thing: Pascal keeps going back to prison! He visits twice a week to preach and distribute Bibles. On Fridays he brings huge pots of vegetable soup, because he found that the prisoners were dying of malnutrition. Many had been jailed for stealing food- they were hungry before they went in.!"

The Chileans look around at each other. This story is hitting close. Ron continues.

"Pascal shows the difference Christ can make in a person's life. When you walk out of prison, you'll probably want to erase it from your mind. But Pascal couldn't do that. He believed God wanted him to go back, to share God's love that he found in that stinking, crowded room."

After the story, the Chilean prisoners, obviously moved, break out in loud applause. Ron continues, telling story after story of people who have met Christ behind bars. Then the members of the congregation speak.

One of the band members, a short, wiry man with a thick scar running across his left cheek, speaks first. "They used to think I was so dangerous that they kept me in chains. And I'll tell you why I started going to prison church- I was looking for an escape hole!" Everyone laughs, even the guards. "But there I found true freedom in Christ, not just a way to escape."

Another prisoner limps to the front. He explains that he lost his leg and most of his bowels in a shooting accident in an Argentine prison. He became a Christian in 1985, he says. Shortly after that he located the man who had killed his brother. "Before, I would have killed that man," he says. "But with Christ in my heart, I was able to forgive him. Now I know I am called to preach to the others here in prison. It's a more important job than being president of General Motors. And with thirty-four years to go on my sentence, I'll have plenty of time!"

The service goes on, gathering emotional steam. Prisoners spontaneously kneel by the rough wooden benches to pray for their fellow inmates. The singing, animated with hand-clapping and foot stomping, gets louder and more boisterous. Other prisoners abandon their basketball games and crowd around the open doorway to see what they are missing. When the foreign visitors leave, amid many hugs and handshakes, all the prisoners stay. They are just getting warmed up.

I can still hear strains of the prisoners' singing as I settle with other visitors around a long rectangular table in the prison warden's office. The warden has asked Ron Nikkel and his guests to meet with the prison's psychologist, sociologist, and social workers. Clearly, we are being shown one of Chile's showcase prisons, with modern facilities and services.

The staff professionals view the effect of Christian faith on the inmates with a spirit of benign tolerance: Sprinkle saltpeter on the inmates' toast to help control their sex drives, and why not add a small dose of religion to help control their tempers. The chaplain and other Prison Fellowship staff members, however, believe their work among inmates can contribute far more. Using statistics and case studies, they demonstrate that no rehabilitation scheme will work unless it takes into account the inmates' spiritual needs.

The discussion ranges along such lines for thirty minutes, at which time the prison warden crosses a tolerance threshold. In every way, the warden fulfills the perfect Hollywood stereotype of a South American military officer. His huge barrel chest serves as a perfect display board for rows and rows of multicolored military ribbons, and his shoulder epaulet sports three stars. Only a bushy mustache breaks up the stony monotony of his shallow face.

When the warden speaks, everyone falls silent. "It doesn't matter to me which faith these prisoners take to," he announces with finality. "But clearly they need to change, and they'll never do it without some outside assistance. Religion may give them the will to change that they could never develop on their own."

As he speaks, we can still hear the prisoners singing in the courtyard chapel. "Chaplain," he continues, "one-third of the men in this facility attend your services. You visit several times a week, but I'm here every day. And I tell you, those men are different. They don't just put on a performance when you come around- they are different than the other prisoners. They have joy. They share with other prisoners. They care about more than themselves. And so I think we ought to do all we can to help this fine work."

The director's statement promptly ends all discussion. All the prison professionals nod their agreement. As we leave the prison, the worship service is finally breaking up. The prisoners are marching around the exercise yard in twin columns, singing hymns to the beat of drums and tambourines. I look at my watch- two hours have passed since the service began.

The taxi downtown Santiago takes a long, circuitous route, and as we ride, Ron reflects on his day at the prison. "It never fails to get to me, no matter how many prisons I visit," he says. "To see human beings in such miserable conditions, and yet praising God. In their faces you can see a joy and love like I've encountered nowhere else. I wish some of the dispirited Christians back in North America and Europe could travel with me and see the difference Christ can make in a person's life. God chooses the weak and foolish things of the world to confound the wise and mighty."

Later, towards the end of their time together, Yancey and Nikkel have another discussion. Yancey writes some people try to prove the truth of the gospel in the halls of academia, battling over apologetics and theology. Others compare the size and force of Christianity against the great religions of the world. Ron Nikkel says he just keeps going to prisons. There he finds the final testing area for forgiveness and love and grace. There he finds whether Christ really is alive.

I ask Ron to think back to the worst setting he'd ever seen. I took this assignment to see how faith survives among people who are pressed to the limits. In the dismal prisons we had visited in Chile and Peru, who could dispute the joy we found among inmates there? But did the pattern hold true around the world? Had he ever found a place of absolute despair, with no crack of hope?

Ron thought for a moment and then told me about the time he and Chuck Colson visited a maximum-security prison in Zambia. Their "guide," a former prisoner named Nego, had described a secret inner prison built inside to hold the very worst offenders. To Nego's amazement, one of the guards agreed to let him show the facility to Chuck and Ron.

"We approached a steel, cage-like building, covered with wire mesh. Cells line the outside of the cage, surrounding a 'courtyard' fifteen by forty feet. Twenty-three hours of each day the prisoners are kept in cells so small they cannot all lay down at once. Nego had spent twelve years in those cells.

"When we approached the inner prison, we could see sets of eyes peering at us from a two-inch space under the steel gate. And when the gates swung open, it revealed squalor unlike I have seen anywhere. There were no sanitation facilities-in fact; the prisoners were forced to defecate in their food pans. The blazing African sun heated up the steel enclosure unbearably. I could hardly breathe in the foul, stifling atmosphere of that place. How could human beings possibly live in such a place? I wondered.

"And yet, here is what happened when Nego told them who we were. Eighty of the one hundred and twenty prisoners went to the back wall and assembled in rows. At a signal, they began singing- hymns, Christian hymns, in beautiful four-part harmony. Nego whispered to me that thirty-five of those men had been sentenced to death and would soon face execution.

"I was overwhelmed by the contrast between their peaceful, serene faces and the horror of their surroundings. Just behind them, in the darkness, I could make out an elaborate charcoal sketch drawn on the wall. It showed Jesus, stretched out on a cross. The prisoners must have spent hours working on it. And it struck me with great force, the force of revelation, that Christ was there with them, sharing their suffering and giving them joy enough to sing in such a place.

"I was supposed to speak to them, to offer inspiring words of faith. But I could only mumble a few words of greeting. They were the teachers, not I."

Amen

GAZING AT CHRIST FROM A JAIL CELL

Philippians 2:1-13

*If then there is any encouragement in Christ, and consolation
from love, any sharing of the Spirit, and compassion and
sympathy, make my joy complete: be of the same mind, having
the same love, being in full accord and of one mind. Do nothing
from selfish ambition or conceit, but in humility regard others
as better than yourselves. Let each of you look not to your own
interests, but to the interests of others.
Let the same mind be in you as that was in Christ Jesus,*

*who, though he was in the form of God, did not regard equality
with God as something to be exploited, but emptied himself,
taking the form of a slave, being born in human likeness.
And being found in human form, he humbled himself and
became obedient to the point of death- even on a cross.*

*Therefore God, so highly exalted him and gave him the name
that is above every name, so that at the name of Jesus every knee
should bend, in heaven and on earth and under the earth, and
every tongue should confess that Jesus Christ is Lord, to the glory
of God, the Father.*

*Therefore, my beloved, just as you have always obeyed me, not in
my presence, but much more now in my absence, work out your
own salvation, with fear and trembling; for it is God who is at
work in you enabling you both to will and to work for his good
pleasure.*

Meditation[1]

(Traveling through this adventure called life: Fall 1999)

In the meditation, *A Message from Paul*, I concluded by re-telling Ron Nikkel's account of visiting a prison in Zambia in a setting which would be the last place one would expect to find hope that stems form the Christian faith. And we heard of the image of Jesus in that jail, drawn on the wall in charcoal. With his hands stretched out on a cross. And the revelation that Christ was there sharing in their suffering and giving them joy enough to sing.

One can only wonder, yet I am fairly certain, that at times those men might find themselves gazing at that drawing of Christ. Or perhaps if they could not get close enough to see that picture through the many bodies crammed into such a small place, they might close their eyes, and the image of that drawing would enter in.

In a very similar way, the feel of this passage from the second chapter of Philippians is also the image of Paul gazing at Jesus from a jail cell. Most Biblical scholars believe that we have Paul quoting an ancient Christian hymn.[1]

There are three questions that come to mind from this hymn, 1) what does the hymn say? 2) what does Paul say by quoting the hymn? and, 3) what is the function of the hymn?

First, as Fred Craddock puts it, the hymn notes, "the central event in the drama of salvation is an act of humble service." It recounts the event and story of Christ, the pre-existence/existence/post-existence. Moving from Christ who emptied himself and obeyed God and glorified God.[2]

Second, it appears that Paul is using this hymn as a means of reminding the church of Philippi what is the foundation of their gathering. In other words, why do they gather in

[1] Fred B. Craddock, *Philippians: Interpretation A Bible Commentary for Teaching and Preaching* (John Knox Press: Atlanta) 1985, p. 39.
[2] Ibid, p. 40-42.

Christ's name? It is within this notion that Paul is attempting to promote unity within the church. Notice that in verse 2, which shortly precedes the hymn in verses 6-11, Paul writes, "be of the same mind, having the same love, being in full accord and of one mind."

This being of one mind does not refer to agreeing on everything but rather to having a common attitude and orientation. In this regard, a common unity is found in the One who humbled himself and seeking to have the "same mind in you that was in Christ Jesus."

Here again, Paul is writing words of encouragement to the church. Seeking to unify the church and inspire them to continue being partners in the faith. For the church to continue to be God's people in their place and time.

Finally, as I noted earlier, I feel the function of the hymn is like Paul gazing at Christ from a jail cell. One's surroundings can be dire yet nothing can stop Paul or us from using one's minds eye and imagination to be free in Christ. Free enough to have Christ fill Paul's heart with joy, hope and expectation!

The litany, *The Humanity of Christ*, has a similar function to me of gazing at Christ. This litany uplifts a variety of images that occurs and evolves for the Christian community, developing a diversity wedded together through a common point on which our many gazes are cast.

<u>The Humanity of Christ</u>
O good Jesus, Word of the Father:
Convert Us.
O good Jesus, Son of Mary:
Make us obedient.
O good Jesus, Prince of Peace:
Give us peace.
O good Jesus, model of patience:
Help us to persevere.
O good Jesus, meek and humble of heart:

Help us become like you.
O good Jesus, our Redeemer:
Save us.
O good Jesus, the true Way:
Direct us.
O good Jesus, eternal Truth:
Instruct us.
O good Jesus, Life everlasting:
Make us alive in you.
O good Jesus, our Support:
Strengthen us.
O good Jesus, our Mediator with the Father:
Reconcile us.
O good Jesus, Physician of the soul:
Heal us.
O good Jesus, our Judge:
Absolve us.
O good Jesus, our King:
Govern us.
O good Jesus, our Sanctification:
Sanctify us.
O good Jesus, Living Bread from heaven:
Fill us.
O good Jesus, Father of the prodigal:
Receive us.
O good Jesus, joy of the soul:
Refresh us.
O good Jesus, our Helper:
Assist us.
O good Jesus, our Protector:
Defend us.
O good Jesus, our Hope:
Sustain us.
O good Jesus, Fountain of life:
Cleanse us.

O good Jesus, our Last End:
Let us come to you.
O good Jesus, our Glory:
Glorify us. Amen.[3]

As you looked at, *The Humanity of Christ*, what images or stanzas struck you the most? Are there words that you have felt from the inside out? Are there words that you might want to get a highlighter and mark?

Or what images or stanzas seem vague or distant? Words that might create an interesting image but as yet no substance. Perhaps we might even have a small desire to get an eraser and erase them. Though it would be much wiser to get a pencil and lightly draw a line through those words for one never knows how experience, life and the nurturing of one's faith might unwrap bountiful new gifts of wonder and insight.

Perhaps if you look over this litany later today, or during the week, or perhaps quite a ways down that road, what stanza or words might you want to add? As you gaze at Christ or have had Christ made known to you in the past (perhaps even from a prison we might have dwelt in for a time) only to have God's spirit revive and awaken us.

Let us spend some time as we go forth gazing at Christ.

Amen

[3] Kyrie Eleison, *The Wideness of God's Mercy: Litanies to Enlarge Our Prayer: Volume Two: Prayers for the World*, (The Seabury Press) 1985, p. 43-44.

LIVING THE GOSPEL:
PARTNERS IN CHRIST

Philippians 4:1-9

Therefore, my brothers and sisters, whom I love and long for, my joy and crown, stand firm in the Lord in this way, my beloved.

I urge Euodia and I urge Syntyche to be of the same mind in the Lord. Yes, and I ask you also, my loyal companion, help these women, for they have struggled beside me in the work of the gospel, together with Clement and the rest of my co-workers, whose names are in the book of life.

Rejoice in the Lord always; again I say, rejoice. Let your gentleness be known to everyone.
The Lord is near. Do not worry about anything, but in everything by prayer and supplication with thanksgiving let your requests be made known to God.
And the peace of God, which surpasses all understanding, will guard your hearts and your minds in Christ Jesus.

Finally, beloved, whatever is true, whatever is honorable, whatever is just, whatever is pure, whatever is pleasing, whatever is commendable, if there is any excellence and if there is anything worthy of praise, think about these things.

Keep on doing the things that you have learned and received and heard and seen in me, and the God of peace will be with you.

Meditation

(Traveling through this adventure called life: Fall 1999)

This is the final part of what has developed into a meditation series based on Paul's letter to the church at Philippi. A letter that Paul wrote from a jail cell.

The first thing that needs to be done is to address Euodia and Syntyche, two women at the church. This is important because it gives us a little window into Paul's attitude towards women in the church. (An issue that remains controversial.) And the result of such an endeavor might have some surprises.

First, we must note that Paul is addressing two women who are leaders within the church. These two women seem to be having some type of conflict. (The specifics of which we do not know.) Second, Paul is not trying to embarrass these women. These women are friends and associates, fellow workers with Paul. They have worked side by side in common suffering, joys and faith in the sharing of the gospel of Jesus Christ. Finally, Paul mentions these two in a letter to be read by the church in worship because he expects the church to help with the healing. For as Fred Craddock concludes, "For all of the dispute about Paul's attitude towards women, they are visibly and significantly present in his references to associates in ministry. Women preached and prayed in Paul's churches (I Corinthians 11:5) and their names are many in Paul's remembrances of a lifetime of shared service (Romans 16:1-16). In fact, Luke says the church at Philippi was begun when Paul went to a place of prayer and 'spoke to the women who had come together'" (Acts 16:13).[1]

With this complete, we can turn to Paul's main point within this passage and, in a way, throughout this letter. Paul

---

[1] Fred B. Craddock, *Philippians: Interpretation A Bible Commentary for Teaching and Preaching*, (John Knox Press: Atlanta) 1985, p. 69-71.

talks about the characteristics of the Christian community. How will their identity be known from their surrounding community?

How will they "shine like the stars to the world" (Philippians 2:15)?

This is one of the central messages of the letter Philippians. Encouragement to live the gospel and for the church to continue being partners in Christ.

To do this, Paul gazes at Jesus from a jail cell, and in so doing, models and encourages the Philippi church to do the same. This focus is found everywhere in this letter! Philippians 4:7 reads, "And the peace of God, which surpasses all understanding will guard your hearts and your minds in Jesus Christ." Philippians 2:5, which is immediately followed by the Christ hymn that we looked at in the meditation *Gazing at Christ from a Jail Cell* reads, "Let the same mind be in you that was in Christ Jesus". And again, during the initial prayer and greeting found in Philippians 1:9-11, "And this is my prayer, that your love may overflow more and more with knowledge and full insight to help you determine what is best, so that in the day of Christ you may be pure and blameless, having produced the harvest of righteousness that comes through Jesus Christ for the glory and praise of God."

By gazing at Christ, we learn of and are drawn to God, and we also know the reality of the living Spirit! Therefore, we can experience and know God at all times, being the source of hope; sustaining us, and moving us toward action. Even in the most difficult times. Even in a jail cell. Even in our suffering (which God does not cause but rather empowers us to endure; grow and perhaps learn from our suffering to then be more able to serve others in their difficult times and loss.)

This focus is everywhere throughout this letter. One more example, though not the last, comes from Philippians 4:23, "The grace of the Lord Jesus Christ be with your spirit."

To conclude, and to my reading, Philippians has three main messages. First, Paul redefining the nature of suffering, thus Christ is present and recognized. Thus there is hope and meaning in all situations. Second, gazing at Christ. And, third, encouragement to live the gospel and be partners in Christ.

We are told how to do this (Philippians 4:4-7) "Rejoice in the Lord always; again I say rejoice. Let your gentleness be known to everyone. The Lord is near. Do not worry about anything but in everything by prayer and supplication with thanksgiving let your requests be made known to God. And the peace of God, which surpasses all understanding will guard your hearts and minds in Christ Jesus."

These realities produce a wonderful diversity! It does not produce the same vision of Christ or subsequent actions. But the focus of one's gaze, Jesus Christ, is the same. And from this common point of gazing there can be unity within diversity through Christ and in love.

Further, the character of the community and those who make up the community is to be the same whether they are experiencing external opposition from their surrounding community or they are experiencing internal rumblings within the church.

Therefore, "Keep on doing the things that you have learned and received and heard and seen in me, and the God of peace will be with you" (Philippians 4:9). "And my God will fully satisfy every need of yours according to his riches in glory in Christ Jesus. To our God and Father be glory forever and ever. Amen" (Philippians 4:19-20).

WHENEVER I AM WEAK, THEN I AM STRONG

2 CORINTHIANS 12: 2-10

I know a person in Christ
who fourteen years ago was caught up to the third heaven-
whether in the body I do not know; God knows.

And I know that such a person- whether in the body or out of the
body I do not know; God knows- was caught up into Paradise
and heard things that are not told, that no mortal is permitted
to repeat. On behalf of such as one I will boast, except of my
weaknesses.
But if I wish to boast, I will not be a fool, for I will be speaking
the truth.

But I refrain from it, so that no one may think better of me
than what is seen in me or heard from me, even considering the
exceptional character of the revelations.

Therefore, to keep me from being too elated, a thorn was given
me in the flesh, a messenger of Satan to torment me, to keep me
from being too elated.

Three times I appealed to the Lord about this, that it would
leave me, but he said to me, "My grace is sufficient for you, for
power is made perfect in weakness."

So, I will boast all the more gladly of my weaknesses, so that the
power of Christ may dwell in me. Therefore I am content with
weaknesses, insults, hardships, persecutions, and calamities for
the sake of Christ;

for whenever I am weak, then I am strong.

Meditation

(Traveling through this adventure called life: Summer 2000)

This passage written by the apostle Paul is both difficult and fascinating. This is true because the meaning of two of the most intriguing verses is difficult to pinpoint precisely. Thus, it leaves much for our imaginations to ponder.

The first verse is the experience that Pail is talking about that occurred to him some fourteen years ago when he was (as Paul puts it) "caught up to the third heaven- whether in body or out of body I do not know; God knows."

The second verse is when Paul writes about a thorn given me in the flesh.

Our imaginations must fill in these gaps because there is not enough internal evidence, nor is there a general consensus among scholars to what exactly Paul is talking about.[1] What this means is that 2 Corinthians and other Biblical letters do not tell us precisely the answers. This would be internal evidence. Trying to locate (sort of like a detective) where Paul might have talked about these things in other places in 2 Corinthians and then moving out to the other letters.

Looking for internal evidence can be an extremely helpful tool to our Biblical reading. For many times we can learn a great deal in this way that then makes a passage lighten up in new ways. Where we are able to get closer to what Paul was thinking when he wrote. Further, by using internal evidence we are able to address difficult passages that can turn Paul's message upside down and backwards if read all by it-self. (The classic example of this is Paul's view of women and leadership roles in the church. There are numerous references to Paul talking about and applauding the work of women (many times spoken by name) in the early Christian churches and only

---

[1] Footnotes found in *New Revised Standard Version: The Oxford Annotated Bible: An Ecumenical Study Bible* (Oxford University Press: New York) 1994, p. 260 NT.

one passage where Paul makes a statement within a particular conflict situation (where worship was being disturbed) that a few women be quiet).

Obviously we can see the benefit of broadening our reading to include all internal evidence in this situation.

A second strategy is to find out what scholars who have the benefit of much study and many times are able to read Paul in his original language of Greek have to say. Many times this can also bear much fruit. Reading a passage in its original language can highlight underlying ideas or imagery that is evident in the original text but is difficult to maintain within a translation. This kind of investigating can be done by reading commentaries written about certain books of the Bible or that try and trace Paul's thought development on a particular idea as the *Spirit* worked with him and he developed that idea more thoroughly in various letters.

However, within both of this chapter's difficult verses these efforts do not give us much. We cannot know conclusively what Paul's experience or (as I like to call it "God-incident" was). Did Paul have some type of near death experience (to use a modern day expression)? Or is Paul referring in some way to the Damascus road and his conversion (Acts 9:1-20)? Could it be that Paul is referring to none of the above but rather to a personal experience he has shared with few?

We do not know. It could be none of the above. And here is where our own experiences and imaginations enter into the picture. For we must fill in the gaps ourselves. Therefore the passage can meet us in personal ways. It can lead to new insights as each person meets the passage from his or her experience base and then shares the insights produced with others.

Let me give an example. For over five years now I have been privileged to do what I get to do as a pastor. And since we are all in some form of ministry we get to experience unique struggles and blessings of faith. One of the blessings I have experienced is that on occasion people (for whatever reason) might feel more comfortable talking about their "God-incidents" to a pastor.

In this way, on three different occasions, I have had persons share with me near-death experiences. And each sharing has been a blessing. As the person has shared a gift of one's faith experience so that another can now get a small taste of it. Each experience has left me feeling in awe of God and assured as one person put it through tear filled eyes, the emphatic nodding of their head and the awesome feel of God's living presence that "heaven is real".

Therefore, while others might have their imaginations drift to something completely different; each time I read this passage, mine returns to these experiences. And the free sharing (never forced) of where our imaginations might drift is a benefit to all.

A very similar thing happens with Paul's reference to a thorn in the flesh. Is he referring to some type of physical wound that persistently acts up over the years? Is he talking about some type of spiritual struggle or question that he has encountered time and time again within his faith journey? Or is he referring to a long-term emotional struggle? Perhaps in modern terms we would call it something like depression or mood swings. Again we do not know conclusively.

Therefore, again we are invited to use our own experience base and imagination to meet the text in a personal way. Realizing that we cannot limit or own a text like this. Rather a text like this can become a walking companion and grow with us as we grow and develop.

Next, let us turn to a few insights that Paul makes that we *can* grasp with much greater certainty for they are *spirit-filled* truths that are able to transcend time and location.

First, there is the observation that success, which can lead to personal boasting, can become a barrier to one's faith development.

How often can we see the struggles of success? Regardless of where this might occur. We see these types of struggles in the business world, entertainment industry, sports world, even within the church. It doesn't seem to matter. When personal success can lead to personal boasting, that then changes a person to develop more and more of an inward vision of the world that concentrates on self.

While Paul is challenging us to maintain an outward vision. Clearly "success" (whatever that might mean) is applauded by Paul. Yet it is the type of success that maintains an outward vision towards others; that pays special attention to the poor and outcast; and ultimately points both self and others to God. This is what Paul is talking about. For it is this type of vision that leads to personal and communal wholeness and happiness.

Finally, I wanted to spend a few moments on the verses "My grace is sufficient for you, for power is made perfect in weakness" and then a little later that talks about "whenever I am weak for the sake of Christ; then I am strong."

It is important to say right up front that this is not saying we are to seek out weakness, insults, hardships, persecutions and calamities. However, it is saying that if and when they might find us (which can be a reality in life) then a person of faith can grow and use them as a source of hope and strength for others.

How often is it that people can be drawn to places where they are able to use the struggles they might have known to benefit others and in doing so benefit themselves as well? Think of persons who are or have taken long-term care of an ill loved one and what they might have inspired through their actions in others or are able to give now that the long-term care of another has ended.

Think of the daily care required for a special needs child who grows to be a special needs adult. And how healing can occur when a person opens themselves up and shares the pain and struggles as well as the joys and small triumphs they have known with others who might be walking daily in similar shoes.

This kind of healing and growth occurs in groups when persons are willing to enter or at times re-enter into times of weakness, pain or grief and then turn this experience into an engine that helps and heals others. And in a strange way it can also lead to the continued healing and growth of the one who has been willing to open their weaknesses.

And Paul writes, "For whenever I am weak, then I am strong."

As I was developing this meditation my mind wandered time and time again to an experience of a person's faith and willingness to expose their weakness and a difficult lived through situation.

It occurred about five and a half years ago around the time that I began serving at a two-point charge in Ohio. A woman contracted a rare disease shortly before her 56th birthday. A disease that stumped all doctors for nearly a week. An illness that would completely paralyze the person except for the ability to blink her eyes for nearly four weeks. (Until God was able to work through the gifts of the mind as doctors were able to determine a diagnosis Guillian-Barre and then be able to use the miracles of modern medicine, which would ultimately lead to a restoration of health.)

How easy might it be for this person to want to run away from this extremely difficult time in her life? A time when she was completely in the need and care of others and her human weakness was so exposed.

How tempting it must have been to simply want to turn the page in this chapter of her life and never talk about it again?

Yet that is not what this woman has done. Instead she has offered, on more than one occasion, to "re-enter" into this experience for the benefit of another. For on more than one occasion she has accepted the invitation of others to visit with another and their family who are going through the same thing.

To enter into what must be a frightening situation since all parties would not have met before. A situation that is bound to stir up difficult memories, for by simply walking in the room, smiling, saying a kind word and sharing that she once was in that exact same situation, God's living hope is restored.

And God's living hope leads to various types of healing and wholeness.

Amen

THE WEDDING AT CANA

John 2:1-11

On the third day
there was a wedding in Cana of Galilee, and the mother of Jesus
was there.

Jesus and his disciples had also been invited to the wedding.
When the wine gave out, the mother of Jesus said to him,
"They have no more wine."

And Jesus said to her,
"Woman, what concern is that to you and me?
My hour has not yet come."

His mother said to the servants,
"Do whatever he tells you."

Now standing there were six stone jars for the Jewish rites of
purification, each holding twenty or thirty gallons.

Jesus said to them,
"Fill the jars with water."
And they filled them to the brim.

He said to them,
"Now draw some out and take it to the chief steward."
So they took it.

When the steward tasted the water that had become wine, and
did not know where it came from (though the servants who had
drawn the water knew), the steward called to the bridegroom
and said to him,

John Ruiz

"Everyone serves the good wine first, and then the inferior wine after the guests have become drunk. But you have kept the good wine until now."

Jesus did this,
the first of his signs, in Cana of Galilee, and revealed his glory;
and his disciples believed in him.

Meditation

(Traveling through this adventure called life: January 2001 shortly before I wrote the meditation For We Are One Body In Christ.)

The gospel of John is a gospel of life and love. And one of my favorite images for the gospel is the image of a choir. In the gospel of John we get to meet all of these fascinating people who, each in their own way, sing about God revealed through the Son, Jesus Christ. In this way, each voice adds to the chorus and to the whole. And at the same time it can be helpful to focus on the individual voices, so that we can think about and learn from each unique voice. Finally, in this passage we hear for the first time from Mary, the mother of Jesus. We can hear Mary's witness a second time much later in the gospel of John at the cross of Jesus (John 19:17-27). However, in this meditation, I am going to focus on this first meeting at the wedding feast at Cana.

This is a passage that talks about Jesus' self-disclosure. In other words it is a passage that talks about who Jesus is. Jesus is the Son of God and through and in Jesus God has done and is doing something marvelous for the entire world. This point is emphasized with Jesus' response to his mother Mary's request when he replies, "My hour has not yet come." However, Mary simply replies to this statement by quietly telling the servants to do whatever Jesus tells them to do.

It is this act of Mary that I wanted to concentrate on. For Mary demonstrates a profound belief in Jesus. And this belief would lead to the increased belief of the disciples. Verse 11 reads, "Jesus did this, the first of his signs, in Cana of Galilee, and revealed his glory; and his disciples believed in him."

What does it mean to believe in someone? Really believe in that someone. And what difference can it make?

This is the question that I believe Mary presents to us in this passage of a wedding that takes place in Cana.

What does it mean to believe in someone and what difference can it make?

Anne Sullivan believed in Helen Keller. In the face of unthinkable odds and in opposition to everyone around her she clung to her belief in Helen. That in Helen there was the spark of something beyond her current state of being. That God created something in her that a childhood disease had taken away, and all Helen needed was someone to help her get it back out for all to see. It was Anne's unflinching belief in Helen that would ultimately hold the key to a whole new way of life for her and a whole new way that we all see and understand people with disabilities or what I prefer calling people with various increased challenges to life.

Anne Sullivan might be a logical example, yet these types of people and these situations occur all the time. Recently, I found this article in Newsweek written by Jean Katzenberg that talks about an experience she had in an article titled, "Teaching a Child, Changing a Life."[1]

Katzenberg writes, Annie was vastly different from the other students I tutor in reading at an inner-city grade school. Usually the kids are glad for a break from the classroom, a chance to be given one-on-one attention by a sympathetic listener. Not Annie. At age 6 years old, she was a waif of a child dressed in hand-me-downs, and she couldn't wait to get away from me. "You're in for quite a challenge," the social worker warned me. "She's missed too many days of first grade because her family keeps moving from apartment to apartment. It's a major effort for her to simply get dressed and go off to school, let alone learn anything once she gets there."

Though I met with Annie twice a week, it was a real struggle to get past the thicket that kept her away from me. She would look at me with unseeing eyes, scarcely answering questions. Sometimes she would shift her stare, gaze across

[1] Jean Katzenberg, Newsweek "Teaching a Child, Changing a Life", January 15, 2001, p. 12.

the room and say, "I want to get back to class." Of course I let her go, even after a short session, I knew there was no point in forcing things if I wanted her to look forward to our time together.

Then one day she mentioned her little brother, who I quickly realized was the light of her life. This was the opening I had been looking for.

"Let's put his name in this blue journal," I said. "It's yours." And I wrote ANNIE on the cover. "Tell me how you spell your brother's name." She suddenly grabbed the pen and printed the letters J,O,E,Y. "Joey," she said. "Joey, I love Joey." And she drew a heart on the top. From then on when we met, she told me more about Joey, and I carefully wrote down what she said. As happens with so many children, she could read most of it back. They were her words, and they meant a lot to her. After that day we met nine more times. For our last session, Annie came in proudly sporting a badge her teacher had given her with the word READER inscribed on it.

During my 25 years as a first-grade teacher and seven years as a volunteer tutor, I have worked with many students like Annie who are behind their classmates in reading skills- and I found that I can help almost every child learn. Annie's teacher made an enormous contribution, but she- like other teachers- couldn't always give so much personal time to one child. That's why there's a need for tutors who can reach the students facing the most difficulties. How? By becoming a friend, searching for what they truly care about- their families, pets, hobbies- and then using that knowledge to help them learn to read. That's what I do. By seeing feelings expressed on paper, my kids learn a solid base of vocabulary. The process also builds trust, since I make it clear that I will not grade them or reveal to others what they say.

It helps if I smile and nod my head in agreement when they read the words correctly.

Later, Katzenberg continues, I was deeply moved by Annie's rhapsodic writing about Joey. "Oh, Joey, I love you more than anybody in the whole wide world!" she wrote in her blue book one day.

With the help of a tutor, a child's passion for someone or something can spark real interest in the written word. Annie could read by the time our sessions were over, but she asked for one last meeting with me so she could finish the passage about Joey and show the journal to her mother.

"I will care for you in my life," she read, her eyes shining. "And I'll respect you and make you be smart, and I will never let you get out of my dreams come true, and I will love you for ever and ever and ever."

Reading this article reminded me of my days as a teacher and later a tutor. And it reminded me of my Educational Theory class at Ohio Dominican College in Columbus, Ohio some 12 years ago.

In that class we were taught two truths that I will never forget and have not found a single situation where these did not apply.

We were taught that for a person to learn (a child or a person of any age) two things needed to occur.

First, the person has to have a reason to learn. These reasons to learn can vary and at one point the common theory was called Tabula Rosa. The theory that children innately have reasons and desires to learn, and the art of the teacher or institution is to simply get out of the way and allow these innate desires to surface.

The Tabula Rosa theory has proven to be totally and utterly incorrect. We simply are not born with innate reasons and desires to learn. Therefore reasons must be provided. And a reason that can develop from a Christian perspective is that all persons are created in the image of God. Therefore, the development of our God given gifts and talents praise God. And as we use these gifts and talents in some way to serve others, or help another grow or help society in some way, then we are functioning in some small way as salt for the world (Matthew 9:13).

The second thing needed for a person to learn was a trusted adult or mentor. That at some point in a child's development this type of person was needed. They might not need that person at all times, and for some fortunate people, there may have been many people who fulfilled this role in their lives. Yet at some point there was someone.

Someone the child was drawn too and simply believed in them.

It could be anyone; a parent, a coach, a teacher, a tutor, a co-worker, a friend, a grandparent, a pastor or clergy person, a scout leader, a figure from history, Jesus…

It could be anyone.

May we all praise, God.

Amen

JESUS' MISSION

Luke 4:14-21

*Then Jesus filled with the power of the Holy Spirit, returned
to Galilee, and a report about him spread through all the
surrounding country.
He began to teach in their synagogues and was praised by
everyone.*

*When he came to Nazareth, where he had been brought up, he
went to the synagogue on the Sabbath day, as was his custom.*

*He stood up to read, and the scroll of the prophet Isaiah was
given to him.
He unrolled the scroll and found the place where it is written:*

*"The Spirit of the Lord is upon me, because he has anointed me
to bring good news to the poor.
He has sent me to proclaim release for the captives and recovery
of sight for the blind, to let the oppressed go free, to proclaim the
year of the Lord's favor."*

*And he rolled up the scroll, gave it back to the attendant, and sat
down.
The eyes of all in the synagogue were fixed on him.*

*Then he began to say to them,
"Today this scripture has been fulfilled in your hearing."*

Meditation

(A Time of Growing Acceptance: Winter 2001)

This passage from the gospel of Luke helps us to answer the question of Jesus' mission and to consider the whole concept of a vision. Whether we are talking about an individual vision or a corporate vision.

It's a very dramatic reading. And just as people's encounters with God through the Son are unique and personal, all adding to the whole, so it is within our Christian scripture, which we call the Bible.

There are a large number of theologians that believe the apostle Paul most succinctly writes about God's mission in and through Jesus Christ in Romans 1:16-17 where Paul writes, "For I am not ashamed of the gospel; it is the power of God for salvation to everyone who has faith, to the Jew first and also to the Greek. For in it the righteousness of God is revealed through faith for faith; as it is written, 'The one who is righteous will live by faith.'"

Within Johannine writings there is large agreement that Jesus' mission is most clearly stated in John 3:16-17 where Jesus states, "For God so loved the world that he gave his only Son, so that everyone who believes in him may not perish but have eternal life. Indeed, God did not send the Son into the world to condemn the world, but in order that the world might be saved through him."

Or later when Jesus simply states, "I am the Way, the Truth and the Life" (John 14:6a).

In the gospel of Luke, Jesus' mission is stated, by quoting the prophet Isaiah. Thus emphasizing God's faithfulness throughout the ages. For it is the Sabbath. Jesus is where he usually is on the Sabbath. He is in the Synagogue. And then he stands up to read from the prophet Isaiah. (In our Bibles it would be the first two verses of Isaiah chapter 61.)

He unrolls the scroll and finds a particular passage and reads…

"The Spirit of the Lord is upon me, because he has anointed me to bring good news to the poor. He has sent me to proclaim release to the captives and recovery of sight to the blind, to let the oppressed go free, to proclaim the year of the Lord's favor."

Then Jesus sits back down. All eyes are upon him. And he simply states, "Today this scripture has been fulfilled in your hearing."

While in Estonia last summer we learned that the meaning of the word Evangelism is simply the proclamation of the good news of Jesus Christ. Is there any wonder why within the Christian community we might answer what that good news is in different ways? Yet at the same time be untied in common devotion to Christ.

The theologian Renita Weems simply writes concerning this passage from the gospel of Luke. "Preaching salvation is the purpose for Jesus' coming into the world."[1]

And this is good news!

A passage like this gets us to consider the whole concept of a mission statement or vision. In the business world, and thankfully within the church and many areas of society the concept of a mission statement has really caught on. In fact, it would be rather commonplace.

Yet in reality the concept of a mission statement or a vision is something of a paradox.

Since we must have a vision to know where we are going. If there is no vision of where one is going then it is most likely that we would be standing still or going around in circles. We must have a vision (some might use the word dream) to know where we are going.

---

[1] Renita J. Weems, *New Proclamation: Year C, 2000-2001: Advent Through Holy Week*, (Fortress Press: Minneapolis) 2000, p. 100.

Therefore, the more detailed and embellished the vision, the greater the opportunity to succeed in reaching that vision. In fact, some would argue that merely the action of having a vision and the work involved in articulating that vision in a detailed and embellished way uplifts the individual or group of people who have uplifted the vision.

Yet, the paradox is that once a vision is articulated in detailed and embellished ways one becomes aware how far away the vision is, and how rarely an individual or group of people actually dwell in the vision.

This would be true for everyone except Jesus who is the Son of God.

Amen

THE TRANSFIGURATION
OF JESUS

Luke 9:28-36

Now about eight days after these sayings Jesus took with him Peter and John and James, and went up on the mountain to pray.

And while he was praying, the appearance of his face changed, and his clothes became dazzling white.
Suddenly they saw two men, Moses and Elijah, talking with him. They appeared in glory and were speaking of his departure, which he was about to accomplish at Jerusalem.

Now Peter and his companions were weighed down with sleep, but since they had stayed awake, they saw his glory and the two men who stood with him.

Just as they were leaving him, Peter said to Jesus, "Master, it is good for us to be here; let us make three dwellings, one for you, one for Moses, and one for Elijah"- not knowing what he said.

While he was saying this, a cloud came and overshadowed them; and they were terrified as they entered the cloud.

Then from the cloud came a voice that said, "This is my Son, my Chosen, listen to him!"

When the voice had spoken, Jesus was found alone. And they kept silent and in those days told no one of any of the things they had seen.

Meditation

(A Time of Growing Acceptance: Winter 2001)

This passage from the gospel of Luke is a passage that I have always found very difficult. It is a text that is read every Sunday before the beginning of Lent. However, I have always tried to avoid it, since for me it was difficult to get a feel for this passage that obviously has spoken often to many people.

In this meditation, we are going to enter into this text and the first thing that needs to be done is to get a sure understanding of what is meant by the word *transfiguration*.

The definition of the word transfiguration in the <u>Webster's New World Dictionary</u> reads, 1) to change the form or appearance; 2) to transform as to glorify.[1]

Many current children's programs and even a movie like X-Men, from last year, play with the idea of transformation. So the idea of a person or thing transforming into something else and in some cases something better is found all over the place in our culture.

Yet, knowing this, at least for me, does not make this passage any easier to grasp.

It wasn't until I was reading a lectionary aid written by the theologian Renita Weems that the significance of the passage began to unfold. (Have you noticed how at times reading or hearing a new idea can open up a whole bunch of new thoughts and insights?)

Weems simply writes that the transfiguration of Jesus is the moment when the main figure in the story is recognized for who he is.[2] Later she continues, "We can only imagine Peter, John and James were forever changed by the experience."[3]

[1] *Webster's New World Dictionary of the American Language: Pocket-Size Edition* (Warner Books) 1984, p.634

[2] Renita J. Weems, *New Proclamation: Year C, 2000-2001: Advent Through Holy Week*, (Fortress Press: Minneapolis) 2000, p. 144.

[3] Ibid, p. 146.

In this way, the transfiguration of Jesus represents the moment that these disciples recognized who Jesus is. That Jesus is the Son of God. And this experience would change them.

Therefore, this passage can stand for that moment or experience when one's understanding of God shifts from a pleasant idea to something real. It is when questions that focus on the question, "Is there a God?" or "Can a person encounter God through Jesus?" become unnecessary since one's reality, one's experience, has revealed the reality of God.

It could be a moment when God's presence was felt in a unique and beautiful way, or a time when a prayer was answered. Some might talk about the birth of a child. Others may talk about a time when the possibility of death was real and yet health is maintained. (I am thinking about a person who described to me an extremely serious car accident where a semi-truck accidentally ran over the hood of their car on the freeway. Yet even though the car was completely totaled they simply unfastened their seat belt and walked away.) Some might describe a near death experience. The list could go on and on. Yet the point is, it is the moment or experience when "proof" of the existence of God is unnecessary since for that person the reality of God is a certainty.

This occurred in John Wesley's life, the founder of the Methodist movement, after hearing a sermon preached, and he describes how he was alone after the service and his heart was strangely warmed.

Today we live in a time when "proof" is usually understood in terms of things we can see or touch or verify scientifically. In this way, some will make long arguments detailing how a prayer answered or a heart strangely warmed cannot be "proven" in these ways. Therefore, arguments will be made that claim these things do not offer evidence of the existence of God and the ability to know God in unique and mysterious ways through the Son, Jesus Christ.

However, I would submit that these types of challenges to the faith are illogical since we accept the existence of things we cannot see or touch or manipulate in scientific ways all the time.

One example…Hope

Hope is a reality. To this there can be no argument. Hope is a reality that, for the Christian, is experienced through the life, death and resurrection of Jesus Christ. In this way, Jesus injects hope into the world for all time and in all places.

Yet hope cannot be seen. Hope cannot be touched. Hope cannot be studied and "proven" in scientific ways. Yet hope is a reality.

It is a reality as important to the human condition as anything can be.

Have you ever entered into a situation where hope is not recognized? Sometimes when we see a commercial seeking funds, for children in another part of the world where survival and living conditions can be very difficult, we might catch a glimpse of a child who does not seem to have hope in their eyes.

The gift of hope is real. It changes and transforms lives. And for the Christian hope is a part of day-to-day existence through the gift of God's Son.

For Peter, John and James the transfiguration of Jesus is that moment that changes everything. Since now all that will occur in the future occurs in light of these disciples knowing who Jesus is.

Yet that doesn't mean that they will always know what to do about it. In fact, we have another example of Peter putting his foot in his mouth. Since he says something to the effect of making a type of monument to mark the location of this incredible event. Somehow Peter is not grasping the full significance of this event at this point.

In fact, the passage tells us that Peter, John and James at this point do not tell others about their experience.

Many times communicating a deep religious experience can be difficult. And pondering the event for a time can be very natural. And sharing that event when the moment seems right or the spirit nudges us can be a wonderful gift for everyone.

This is what Peter, John and James do. The event recorded in the gospel of Luke begins with prayer. "They went with Jesus up on the mountain to pray." Then the scene shifts and they know an intense religious experience. They do not talk about it initially. Yet, we can assume they think about and ponder the event.

And then at a later time, in their case, a time after the resurrection of Jesus Christ, they eventually share their experience for the benefit of others.

Amen

GOD'S STEADFAST LOVE

Luke 19:28-38

After he had said this,
he went on ahead, going up to Jerusalem.

When he had come near Bethphage and Bethany, at the place
called the Mount of Olives, he sent two of the disciples, saying,
"Go into the village ahead of you, and as you enter it you will
find tied there a colt that has never been ridden. Untie it and
bring it here.
If anyone asks you, 'Why are you untying it?' just say this,
'The Lord needs it.'"

So those who were sent departed and found it as he had told
them. As they were untying the colt, the owners asked them,
"Why are you untying the colt?"

They said,
"The Lord needs it."

Then they brought it to Jesus; and after throwing their clocks on
the colt, they sent Jesus on it.

As he rode along, people kept throwing their cloaks on the road.
As he was now approaching the path down from the Mount of
Olives, the whole multitude of the disciples began to praise God
joyfully with a loud voice for all the deeds of power they had
seen, saying,

"Blessed is the king who comes in the name of the Lord!"

Peace in heaven and glory in the highest heaven!"

Luke 22:14-20

When the hour came, he took his place at the table, and the
apostles with him.

He said to them,
"I have eagerly desired to eat this Passover with you before I
suffer;
for I tell you, I will not eat it until it is fulfilled in the kingdom
of God."

Then he took a cup,
and after giving thanks he said,
"Take this and divide it among yourselves;
for I tell you that from now on I will not drink of the fruit of the
vine until the kingdom of God comes."

Then he took a loaf of bread, and when he had given thanks, he
broke it and gave it to them saying,
"This is my body, which is given up for you. Do this in
remembrance of me."

And he did the same with the cup after supper, saying,
"This cup that is poured out for you is the new covenant in my
blood."

Meditation

(A Time of Growing Acceptance: Spring 2001)

Holy Scripture reveals to us the story of God's steadfast love. It tells time and time again of God's love that remains steadfast even when people have turned away. A steadfast love that is perfectly revealed for all to see in and through Jesus Christ.

The first passage is usually read on the Sunday prior to Easter or what is called Palm Sunday. It tells us of Jesus' triumphant welcome into Jerusalem. In fact, the welcome Jesus receives is like a heroes welcome!

People are singing and shouting! Spontaneously, some begin to cut palm branches and wave them in the air. Others begin to take off their cloaks and place them in front of the donkey to walk on. (Almost like a red carpet.) The people are excited and the scene reminds us of the welcoming of a hero!

This brings us to an interesting question. How often de we like to build heroes up only to tear them down if they do not meet up with our expectations? (Whatever that might be.)

Yesterday, I was doing a little channel surfing and came upon the Masters golf tournament. I'll admit that I don't watch much golf on TV. I like to play. Although I am terrible at the game. Anyway, I was watching a little and the announcers kept talking about Tiger Woods. How he was attempting to win his fourth consecutive Major's golf tournament in a row. How we might be watching history in the making!

I guess it worked, because I watched for an hour or so.

Clearly, Tiger Woods was being built up as a hero. However, what happens if he acts in ways that don't meet up to our standards? (Realizing that those standards can vary for each person.)

What happens if he wins? Yet some think he accepts his award in a way that isn't humble enough or perhaps in a way that seems too humble. What happens if he loses? And caught up in the emotion he demonstrates disappointment or anger so some will call him a poor loser. Or if he loses, yet appears to take the loss too much in stride and some complain that he doesn't seem to have a sense of the history of the game.

See how it can work? In such a situation people can only be who they are. And in Jesus' situation he is the Savior of the world.

In Jesus' situation the conflict will turn on different visions of the kingdom. What it will look like and whom it is for.

Many who are cheering as Jesus enters Jerusalem (though not all) will change their tune in a few short days.

They had expected a hero on a white horse that would restore Israel's military might. Instead, they have a man of peace and grace riding on a donkey.

They had expected the restoration of a kingdom that would remind them of the great days of yesteryear and the reign of David. Instead, they have a man who is a teacher; who teaches that the kingdom of God is like a mustard seed (Luke 13:18-19) or a woman who has lost a coin (Luke 15:8-10).

They had expected God to act for them! For the Israelite people! Especially, the ruling class, who had taught and preserved the faith. Even during the difficult years.

Instead, God has acted through his Son. A man who has a special way with the poor and outcasts. The poor and outcasts seem drawn to him. Further, this man teaches in ways that challenge the ruling class. After all, the story he told of the man wounded on a road had a Samaritan who came to his aid (Luke 10:25-37). This is implying that the kingdom of God is open to all. Open even to those people we don't like; like the Samaritans. Open even to our enemies, like the Romans (Luke 6:32-36). Simply open to all...

And in a few short days the cheers of a heroes welcome will change. In less than a week Jesus will carry his cross for you and for me and for the world (Luke 23:26-49).

However, before he will do that there is much to do and much to teach. Some of which occurs in an upper room with his disciples. Where during the traditional Jewish Passover feast Jesus will do something different.

He will take bread, give thanks and break the bread. Later, he will take a cup. He will give thanks and declare that this is the blood of the new covenant! And in so doing Jesus will initiate a new feast and welcome all people, everywhere, throughout history, to join the feast! A feast! A celebration that is already going on! A celebration that reminds us time and time again of Jesus and the saving ways God has acted (and acts) in the world through the Son.

We join in the feast, whenever we partake in Holy Communion.

Later, on this night (which is now called Maunday Thursday) Jesus would go out into a garden and pray. While out in that garden praying, a mob would emerge, led by Judas and Roman soldiers. And Jesus would be arrested (Luke 22:39-54).

He would be falsely accused of crimes, and in a mockery of a trial, he would be condemned to death (Luke 22:55-23:25).

Death on a cross (Luke 23:46).

How quickly things can change. A heroes welcome one day. A cross a few days later.

Yet, Jesus can only be who he is. And God can only be who God is. And God is steadfast love. A steadfast love that is perfectly revealed for all to see in and through Jesus Christ.

And Jesus will pray from the cross, "Father forgive them for they know not what they are doing" (Luke 23:34a).

Truly a hero of salvation for all time...

Amen

West Bend Library

Title: The Simpsons
[videorecording (DVD)] : the
complet
Item ID: 3357003263907
Date due: 7/21/2008,23:59

Questions call 262-335-5151
www.west-bendlibrary.org

West Bend Comm Mem Lib

Title: Living with post traumatic
stress disorder
Date due: 8/11/2008,23:59
Item ID: 33357003206690

Title: War and the soul : healing
our nation's veterans
Date due: 8/11/2008,23:59
Item ID: 33357003253601

Library phone: 262-335-5151
www.west-bendlibrary.org

THE MYSTERY OF THE
RESURRECTION AND THE
TRIUMPH OF HOPE

John 20:1-18

*Early on the first day of the week, while it was still dark, Mary
Magdalene came to the tomb and saw that the stone had been
removed from the tomb. So she ran and went to Simon Peter and
the other disciples, the one whom Jesus loved, and said to them,
"They have taken the Lord out of the tomb, and we do not know
where they have laid him."*

*Then Peter and the other disciple set out and went toward the
tomb. The two were running together, but the other disciple
outran Peter and reached the tomb first. He bent down to look
in and saw the linen wrappings lying there, but he did not go in.
Then Simon Peter came, following him, and went into the tomb.
He saw the linen wrappings lying there, and the cloth that had
been on Jesus' head, not lying with the linen wrappings but rolled
up in a place by itself. Then the other disciple, who reached the
tomb first,also went in, and he saw and believed; for as yet they
did not understand the scripture, that he must rise from the
dead. Then the disciples returned to their homes.*

*But Mary stood weeping outside the tomb.
As she wept, she bent over to look into the tomb; and she saw two
angels in white, sitting where the body of Jesus had been lying,
one at the head and the other at the feet. They said to her,
"Woman, why are you weeping?"*

*She said to them,
"They have taken away my Lord, and I do not know where they
have laid him."*

*When she said this, she turned around and saw Jesus standing
there, but she did not know it was Jesus.*

John Ruiz

Jesus said to her,
"Woman, why are you weeping?
Whom are you looking for?"

Supposing him to be the gardener, she said to him,
"Sir, if you have carried him away, tell me where you have laid
him, and I will take him away."

Jesus said to her,
"Mary!"

She turned and said to him in Hebrew,
"Rabbouni!" (Which means Teacher).

Jesus said to her,
"Do not hold on to me, because, I have not yet ascended to the
Father.
But go to my brothers and say to them, 'I am ascending to my
Father and your Father, to my God and your God.'"

Mary Magdalene went and announced to the disciples,
"I have seen the Lord"; and she told them that
he had said these things to her.

EASTER MEDITATION 2001

There are so many possible places to focus on when encountering a text like this passage and the topic of resurrection. We could focus on Mary Magdalene's side of the story.[1] Or we could focus on God's activity in and through the Son, Jesus Christ. There are many different starting points and in this meditation I am going to focus on the two disciples who race to the tomb of Jesus after Mary Magdalene has reported to them that the stone has been removed.

It is helpful to imagine the scene in our minds. Mary Magdalene has approached the tomb of Jesus to pay her last respects. She has come to grieve. Only she notices as she approaches the tomb that the stone at the entrance has been rolled away. We can only imagine what she might have felt, the despair and the confusion. And she leaves to tell someone what has happened.

This seems reasonable. She rushes to where others were gathered, and the first people she meets are Peter and the other disciple. She tells them what has happened, and these two disciples also have a very reasonable response. They run to see for themselves!

The other disciple must have been faster because he gets to the tomb first. And as someone who does not like to run long distances, I have this wonderful image of Peter gasping for air as he runs to try and keep up with the other disciple.

You see, these two disciples would have been mourning the death of Jesus. Only a few days earlier they had witnessed the false accusation and the brutal death of a man they had come to love. A man they had come to know as a great teacher and a friend. A man they even began to know as Messiah who is the Son of God.

[1] John Ruiz, *A Message of Life and Love: Proclaiming Good News from a Johannine Perspective* (Morris Publishing: Kearney, Nebraska) 2001, p. 66-72.

John Ruiz

So these two disciples had come to console each other in their grief. One a disciple known only as the other disciple (or the beloved disciple) and the other Peter, who was also carrying the burden of a secret, for he had denied Jesus three times before the cock crowed (Matthew 26:69-75 and Mark 14:66-72 and Luke 22:54-62 and John 18:12-27). Had he told anyone at this point? We do not know. We only know that such an experience would add huge amounts of guilt to the grief he was already experiencing.

Then they hear from Mary Magdalene and begin to run to the tomb. Peter is not as fast as the other disciple, so when he approached the tomb, the beloved disciple is standing at the entrance peering in. Peter gets there and does a very Peter like thing. He plunges right in and enters the empty tomb. And he sees the linen and the cloth used on Jesus' head not lying with the linen but rolled up in a place by itself.

And they leave. Struggling to understand what has happened. Struggling to solve the mystery of the empty tomb. Not knowing, at this point, that the mystery of the empty tomb can only be answered through the mystery of the resurrection and God's triumph of hope.

We live in a time in history that likes to think we know a lot. It is one of the characteristics of our culture and the time in history we live in. We want proof before we will give our hearts to the mysteries of life. Therefore for many, in what is sometimes called the "modern" world, the scandal of an empty tomb and the mystery of the resurrection are hard to believe.

However, it is within the pondering of an empty tomb and realization of the mystery of the resurrection that we begin to understand God's freedom and all consuming love. And as a result of these insights we are able to receive gifts God is giving to us and to the world. Since God is mysterious and free we also are free and life itself begins to develop a mysterious and wondrous quality.

Joseph Girzone writes in his book <u>A Portrait of Jesus</u>, "Jesus' love is not superficial or fickle. Friendship doesn't end just because we do stupid things, especially out of our weakness. It's all right! All Jesus' friends limp or are seriously defective in some way. It doesn't bother Him. That is what is so extraordinary about God's love."[2]

Later Girzone writes, "For it is our failings and weaknesses, as humiliating as they are to us, that God uses to accomplish His wonders within us and uses as the engine that drives us to become the instruments of His miracles of grace to others."[3]

These are the insights that Peter will learn and experience from the inside out. For the burden of the guilt that he would carry and the grief that was weighing down his heart would be lifted away through a risen Lord.

This would occur later as Peter is witness to the resurrected Lord and later has an incredible conversation with Jesus on a beach (John 21:1-17).[4] Yet, today, on this day, the healing has already begun. For Peter is left pondering an empty tomb.

What could it mean? What could the linen and neatly rolled up head covering mean? It must have given Peter much to think about. Could it be? The birth of a renewed hope might have begun to flicker within Peter at such a thought.

Could it be?

At a much later time Peter or one of Peter's followers who had come to know Jesus through the testimony of Peter would write these words.[5] They are found within I Peter 1: 3-5, "Blessed be the God and Father of our Lord Jesus Christ!

---

[2] Joseph F. Girzone, *A Portrait of Jesus* (Doubleday: New York, London, Toronto, Sydney, Auckland) 1998, p. 28-29.

[3] Ibid, p. 92-93.

[4] John Ruiz, *A Message of Life and Love: Proclaiming Good News from a Johannine Perspective* (Morris Publishing: Kearney, Nebraska) 2001, p. 85-89.

[5] Luke Timothy Johnson, *The Writings of the New Testament: An Interpretation* (Fortress Press: Philadelphia) 1986, p. 430-441.

By his great mercy he has given us a new birth into a living hope through the resurrection of Jesus Christ from the dead, and into an inheritance that is imperishable, undefiled and unfading, kept in heaven for you."

You see at some point Peter's pondering would bear fruit. And the fruit that he would know from the inside out and proclaim for all to hear "is a new birth into a living hope through the resurrection of Jesus Christ from the dead."

Some might continue to argue that for them this is not proof. For one who has touched or experienced such a living hope such additional proof is needless. For within one's own reality the mystery of the resurrection has begun to add realness, quality and meaning to life.

Yet for the skeptic there remain gifts in pondering such a mystery. To these gifts I would like to add a thought.

Many of us in the "modern" world are influenced by ideas that are around us and we might not even be sure where they come from. One example is the idea, "I think therefore I am." This is actually an idea that comes from the French philosopher Rene Descartes.

This idea "I think therefore I am" is one that has captured the imagination of many an artist. One example is that very famous sculpture of the "Thinking Man" by Rodan. We have probably all seen a model of it at some point. The man sitting, his head propped up on his hand. Thinking…"I think therefore I am."

Believe it or not, the movie, Pokemon 3, works with the same idea. Where a little girl's thought became reality because she thinks them. I had the chance to see the movie last Sunday, and we even get to meet a brand new Pokemon. The Pokemon named Entei who comes to life because the little girl thinks it. (It is amazing how various thoughts and ideas are around us all the time.)

It is here that I would like to add another thought. It is one that has also been around for many, many years, and I recently came in contact with as I was reading a book written by one of our great living theologians. He talked about a need to recapture the idea that "I am therefore I think" in our culture.[6]

I am therefore I think. (It is a very different idea isn't it?) I am therefore I think.

I am (and we are) persons of dignity and worth therefore I think of the dignity and worth of others.

I am (and we are) persons of creativity and imagination therefore I understand the use of my creativity and imagination as a good thing.

I am (and we are) people created in the image of God, and therefore I (and we are) gifts from God to others. Therefore I understand others who are also created in the image of God to be gifts from God.

For Peter it would follow…I am filled with a living hope and the burdens of my guilt and the despair of my grief have been lifted away through the resurrection of Jesus Christ from the dead. Therefore he will see a living hope in all aspects of life and even in death that leads to eternal life and he will seek to share this good news to all people.

Amen

[6] John Paul II, *Crossing the Threshold of Hope* (Alfred A. Knopf: New York) 1994, p. 38.

TRAVELING THROUGH THIS ADVENTURE CALLED LIFE (CONTINUED...)

John 1:1-18

*In the beginning was the Word, and the Word was with God,
and the word was God.*
*He was in the beginning with God. All things came into being
through him, and without him not one thing came into being.*

*What has come into being in him was life, and the life was the
light of all people. The light shines in the darkness, and the
darkness did not overcome it.*

*There was a man sent from God, whose name was John.
He came as a witness to testify to the light, so that all might
believe through him. He himself was not the light, but he came
to testify to the light.*
*The true light, which enlightens everyone, was coming in the
world.*

*He was in the world, and the world came into being through
him: yet the world did not know him. He came to what was
his own, and his own people did not accept him. But to all who
received him, who believed in his name, he gave the power to
become children of God, who were born, not of blood or of the
will of the flesh or of the will of man, but of God.*

*And the Word became flesh and lived among us, and we have
seen his glory, the glory of the father's only son, full of grace and
truth.*

*(John testified to him and cried out,
"This was he of whom I said, 'He who comes after me ranks
ahead of me because he was before me.'")*

John Ruiz

From his fullness we have received, grace upon grace.
The law indeed was given through Moses; grace and truth came
through Jesus Christ.
No one has ever seen God. It is the only Son, who is close to the
Father's heart, who has made him known.

Meditation

At some point while I was writing these meditations, putting together this book and my earlier book, I realized that these meditations had been a source of healing and strength over the years. Further, I came to realize that these things had continued to be sources of healing and strength during unexpected shifts and turns that have occurred in my life. (After all unexpected shifts and turns are just a part of everybody's life.)

In this way, I pray that these writings may offer comfort and peace or healing and strength in some unknown situation or place. Whether this is a situation where one knows what it is like to live swimming upstream or knows and cares for someone who lives life this way. Or if these writings simply meet someone and speak in some way in whatever might be one's current lot in life. As we all continue to travel through this great adventure called life…

Footprints

One night a man had a dream. He dreamed he was walking along the beach with the Lord.
Across the sky flashed scenes from his life, for each scene, he noticed two sets of footprints in the sand; one belonged to him, and the other to the Lord.

When the last scene of his life flashed before him, he looked back at the footprints in the sand. He noticed that many times along the path of his life there was only one set of footprints.
He also noticed that it happened at the very lowest and saddest times in his life.
This really bothered him and he questioned the Lord about it. "Lord, you said that once I decided to follow you, you'd walk with me all the way. But I've noticed that during the most troublesome times in my life, there is only

one set of footprints. I don't understand why when I needed
you most you would leave me."

The Lord replied, "My precious, precious child, I love you
and I would never leave you.
During your times of trial and suffering, when you see only
one set of footprints, it was then that I carried you.[1]

---

[1] The poem *Footprints* was written by Margaret Fishback Powers.

BIBLIOGRAPHY

Anderson, Dennis A. Course Evangelism MN 2604, taught at the Trinity Lutheran Seminary in Columbus, Ohio during the Fall Quarter 1994.

Bishop Minor shared messages at the West Ohio Annual Conference of the United Methodist Church in June 1996.

Bishop Peter Storey shared messages at the Wisconsin Annual Conference of the Untied Methodist Church in June 1998.

Craddock, Fred B. Luke: Interpretation A Bible Commentary for Teaching and Preaching, John Knox Press: Louisville, 1990.

Craddock, Fred B. Philippians: Interpretation A Bible Commentary for Teaching and Preaching, John Knox Press: Atlanta, 1985.

Eleison, Kyrie compiled and adapted by Jeffery W. Rowthorn. The Wideness of God's Mercy: Litanies to Enlarge Our Prayer: Volume Two: Prayers for the World, The Seabury Press, 1985.

Gabarain, Cesareo translated by Gertrude C. Suppe, George Lockwood and Raquel Gutierrez-Achon. The United Methodist Hymnal, The United Methodist Publishing House: Nashville, Tennessee, 1989. (Hymn #344, "Lord, You Have Come to the Lakeshore")

Girzone, Joseph F. A Portrait of Jesus, Doubleday: New York, London, Toronto, Sydney, Auckland, 1998.

John Paul II. Crossing the Threshold of Hope, Alfred A. Knopf: New York 1994.

Johnson, Luke Timothy. The Writings of the New Testament: An Interpretation, Fortress Press: Philadelphia, 1986.

Katzenberg, Jean. Newsweek, "Teaching a Child, Changing a Life", January 15, 2001, p. 12.

Powers, Margaret Fishback. "Footprints".

Ruiz, John. <u>A Message of Life and Love: Proclaiming Good News from a Johannine Perspective</u>, Morris Publishing: Kearney, Nebraska, 2001.

Wallis, Ethel Emily. <u>God Speaks Navajo</u>, Harper Row Publishers: New York, Evanston, London, 1968.

Watley, William D. <u>Sermons From the Black Pulpit</u>, Judson Press: Valley Forge, 1984.

Webster's New Dictionary of the American Language: Pocket-Size Edition, Warner Books, 1984.

Weems, Renita J. New Proclamation: Year C, 2000-2001: Advent Through Holy Week, Fortress Press: Minneapolis, 2000.

Wesley, John. Professor Paul Chilcote read this prayer written by John Wesley during the class DS 380 United Methodism I, in the fall quarter of 1995 at the Methodist Theological School in Ohio.

Yancey, Philip. <u>Finding God in Unexpected Places</u>, Servant Publications: Ann Ardor, Michigan 1997.

<u>The New Oxford Annotated Bible: An Ecumenical Study Bible</u>, Oxford University Press: New York, 1994

<u>The New Revised Bible Standard Version</u>, Thomas Nelson Publishers: Nashville, Burlingame, 1990.

The Student Bible: New International Version

About The Author

John Ruiz is a United Methodist pastor currently serving in Ohio. Ruiz is also the author of *A Message of Life and Love: Proclaiming Good News from a Johannine Perspective.*

Printed in the United States
31395LVS00001B/146